WALKI

—

BOWLAND

WALKING COUNTRY

——————

BOWLAND

Paul Hannon

——————

Hillside

HILLSIDE
PUBLICATIONS
20 Wheathead Crescent
Keighley
West Yorkshire
BD22 6LX

First published 1994
Fully Revised 2006
6th edition 2009

© Paul Hannon 2006, 2009

ISBN 978-1-870141-78-9

Cover illustration: River Hodder, Newton-in-Bowland
Back cover: Brennand Valley, Chipping, Langden Brook
Page One: The Grey Stone of Trough
Page Three: Clougha Pike
(Paul Hannon/Hillslides Picture Library)

The sketch maps in this book are based upon
1947 Ordnance Survey One-Inch maps

Printed in Great Britain by
Carnmor Print
95-97 London Road
Preston
Lancashire
PR1 4BA

CONTENTS

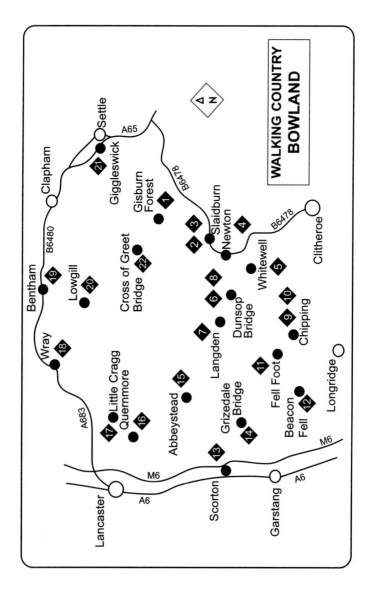

WALKING COUNTRY
BOWLAND

N

INTRODUCTION

The Forest of Bowland covers a vast area of North Lancashire, overlapping into North Yorkshire, and in 1964 some 312 square miles of it were designated an Area of Outstanding Natural Beauty. Bowland is that mass of upland left rather bare on the map of Lancashire: empty on the map, maybe, but very rich on the ground. The broad outer boundaries are delineated by roads linking Lancaster, Settle, Clitheroe, Longridge and Garstang. The actual AONB boundaries extend beyond the bounds of this book, for the mass of Pendle Hill, across the Ribble, is a detached pocket of this AONB. Though perhaps administratively convenient, it is different in character: indeed, coupled with the Ribble Valley from Gisburn down through Clitheroe to Ribchester, that area is sufficiently independent and extensive to merit its own book of walks.

Bowland's two distinct aspects are the great dome of rugged moorland and the softer valley country, with the latter being found predominantly in the south-east of the region. Linking them is the chief river of Bowland, the Hodder, a beautiful, sparkling stream that meanders from high moorland surrounds to gentle pastoral country. It gives us the lovely villages of Slaidburn, capital of Bowland, and Newton, though throughout the region are charming stone villages with much history. In Lunesdale to the north are Wray, Hornby and the Benthams; in Wyresdale to the west are Abbeystead and Scorton; while to the south there is Chipping, sat in its own vale and with its own inimitable character. While the major rivers such as Ribble and Lune certainly bound the area, it is the Hodder that truly belongs to Bowland.

Bowland's isolation is really a myth, for not only does it border the popular Yorkshire Dales and the Fylde Coast (each is within a stone's throw at times), it is highly accessible to the large Lancashire conurbations, and indeed West Yorkshire, while the M6 motorway skirts the very base of the western moors. Strange then, that in these days of congested roads and costly fuel, few of those that tear up either that motorway or the overburdened A65 ever stop to explore Bowland, bound instead for the less subtle charms of the Lake District. Admittedly, Bowland has no real craggy peaks and ridges, no real lakes and mountains, but neither has it reams of eroded paths and masses of dayglo walking groups. What it does boast is both solitude and wildlife - in abundance!

Geologically, Bowland is an outlier of the Pennines, though physically it is entirely separate. Where it does hint at meeting higher ground, it is the contrasting limestone country of the Dales around Settle. Bowland however is predominantly millstone grit, though it does offer its own limestone pockets. While most of the outcrops of more traditional Pennine gritstone country are largely absent, the rocks are certainly in evidence on countless occasions.

Bowland became a royal forest in 1332, and was soon a part of the Duchy of Lancaster, as much still is today. The term 'forest' is of course misleading, relating as it does to the fact that this was for many centuries a deer hunting preserve - though at one time it really would have been tangled in woodland. Today the trees retain their place in the valleys, leaving the open country to be just that - very open. Most of the land is held by vast estates, with United Utilities and the Duke of Westminster staking major claims - each estate extending to more than 20,000 acres.

Today the Bowland hunter's quarry is no longer deer but small birds, and the rolling heather moors are intensively managed for grouse shooting. While the deer of yesteryear may have gone, these shy creatures can again be found, predominantly Sika and Roe: Gisburn Forest is a popular haunt. As Red deer spread further and wider, they too might be glimpsed here again. Bowland's importance to other species is emphasized by the fact that 2004 saw this as the only place in England where the hen harrier was known to hatch, making it a particularly suitable adornment to Bowland's logo.

Of the few motor roads able to negotiate a way across Bowland, mention must be made of the celebrated Trough road. Crossing the old county boundary between Dunsop Bridge via the Trough of Bowland to Wyresdale, on its crest stands the old Grey Stone of Trough. The Pendle witches were brought this way for trial at Lancaster, while today it offers a leisurely route to the coast for Yorkshire and East Lancashire folks going 'through the Trough'.

Bowland's hen harrier

Access to the Bowland countryside

The majority of walks in this guide are on public rights of way with no access restrictions, or long-established access areas and paths. A handful also take advantage of the 2004 implementation of 'Right to Roam'. This new freedom allows more logical routes to be created: such walks are noted in their introduction. Existing access areas and concession paths now largely fall within these vast swathes of Open Country, and on most days of the year you are free to walk responsibly over these wonderful landscapes. Of various restrictions that do pertain, the two most notable are that dogs are normally banned from grouse moors; and also that the areas can be closed to walkers for up to 28 days each year, subject to advance notice being given. Inevitably the most likely times will be from the 'Glorious Twelfth', the start of the grouse shooting season in August, though weekends should largely be unaffected. Further information can be obtained from the Countryside Agency (see page 95), and ideally from information centres. Finally, bear in mind that in springtime (April-June) avoiding tramping over open country, away from paths and tracks would greatly help safeguard the most crucial period for vulnerable ground nesting birds.

Though public transport within the area is limited, decent services skirt the perimeter, striking into most villages. Railway stations are found at Clitheroe, Giggleswick, Settle, Clapham, Bentham, Wennington and Lancaster. Availability of any public transport is mentioned in the introduction to each walk.

Using the guide

Each walk is self contained, with essential information being followed by a concise route description and simple map. Dovetailed in between are notes and illustrations of features along the way. Snippets of information have been placed in *italics* to ensure that the essential route description is easier to locate. The sketch maps serve to identify the location of the routes rather than the fine detail, and whilst the description should be sufficient to guide you around, an Ordnance Survey map is strongly recommended.

To gain the most from a walk, the detail of the 1:25,000 scale Explorer map is unsurpassed. It also gives the option to vary walks as desired, giving an improved picture of your surroundings and the availability of linking paths. Just one map covers all the walks in this book: • *Explorer OL41 - Forest of Bowland & Ribblesdale*
Also useful for planning are Landranger maps 97, 98, 102 and 103.

STOCKS RESERVOIR

START Gisburn Forest   Grid ref. SD 732565

DISTANCE 8¹4 miles (13km)

ORDNANCE SURVEY MAPS
1:50,000
Landranger 103 - Blackburn & Burnley
1:25,000
Explorer OL41 - Forest of Bowland & Ribblesdale

ACCESS Start from North West Water's Stocks Reservoir car park, signed off the B6478 Slaidburn-Tosside road in the Gisburn Forest.

> *Enjoy scenic views over this shapely sheet of water*
> *- bring binoculars to appreciate the birdlife*

This is not the entirely gentle stroll many a reservoir circuit offers - be prepared for some moisture underfoot. Much of this walk coincides with a waymarked water company circular route.

The near-350 acres of Stocks Reservoir were created in 1922 and officially opened in 1932 to supply the Blackpool area, in the process killing off a village and a way of life. Salt was rubbed into the wound by taking the village's name: Stocks-in-Bolland (Bowland's former name) was a modest community, its cottagers served by inn, shop, Post office, school and church. During the construction work a shanty town grew up - far larger than anything luckless Stocks had ever mustered - but now all is gone. Several miles of narrow-gauge railway line were even laid from Tosside to transport materials from the Long Preston road. This extended for many miles beyond the site to the quarries worked for the dam: part of the walk will follow its course. The road climbing away is

School Lane, another poignant reminder of days past at Dale Head. Planting began here in 1949, and in more recent times Forest Enterprise has improved the area by creating more varied habitats and catering for visitors with information boards. The name Gisburn Forest appended to this vast swathe of green is actually a centuries-old name for a former hunting ground.

A broad path heads away from the corner of the car park, along a wallside passing the picnic area on the site of the old church and a short branch path to the bird hide. The main path forges on through a felled area that has been replanted with a variety of broad-leaved trees permitting views over the reservoir. Simply remain on this largely firm path, and reaching a T-junction ignore the right branch and just advance straight on. Passing an old barn,

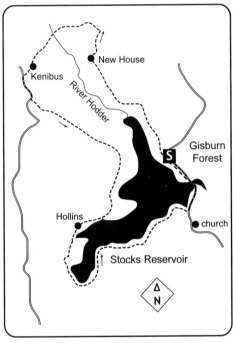

mature plantings have been felled creating further open country and enjoying a good view over the upper Hodder with colourful scenery behind. The broad green path runs to a gate into a green pasture, and a faint, raised green way drops to a stone arched bridge over Hasgill Beck. Across it a good track rises up the field-sides to a barn and shelter belt of trees, all that remain of New House.

The track continues to a stile just above, where pause to look back over Stocks' waters to the great prow of Pendle Hill. The continuing broad track crosses a pasture to a wall at the end, though the actual right of way takes a longer circuit around the top of the pasture before dropping back to rejoin it. From a stile at the end remain on the main track which descends to a gate at the top of Parks Clough. As it turns to run on to Catlow Farm, turn down a green way by the wooded ravine to meet the farm drive. This is followed down to cross the lively young Hodder at Lock Bridge. *Climbing away, look back to appraise the enviable setting of Catlow Farm beneath Hasgill Fell, with the outcrop of Bowland Knotts high above.* The farm road rises to emerge by way of the white-walled Kenibus onto the Bentham road. *Alongside is an old quarry used as part of the supply for building the Stocks dam.*

Turn left, crossing the wooded environs of Hare Clough Beck and on to a bend. Without crossing the cattle-grid use the stile directly ahead, and take a grassy track past a substantial barn. *This is an old road that ran to Stocks village, prior to its watery demise.* After a couple of fields vacate it - as it starts a gentle decline - by an initially less appealing track that sets off through rushes on the right: discerning eyes will see it continue as a contouring green way. *This is the bed of the rail line constructed to transport stone from the recently passed quarry as well as the larger Jumbles Quarry further up-dale (see WALK 22). Just an occasional sleeper remains.*

It is impossible to go astray on this next stage, for aside from one or two moister moments, a super route takes off along the track-bed, featuring an early cutting. Ahead is the great sprawl of the forest again. In time the reservoir appears ahead, and remains in sight for most of the walk. All 'bridges' are down, and the surrounding terrain is largely gone to seed but nevertheless colourful. Simply remain on this route as it chugs along to approach Stocks Fishery, with the dam appearing beyond. Here a firm track bizarrely rises from the water to take over for the short section to the fishery base at Hollins. *This is a popular spot for fish-chasers, with boats for hire and a small fishermans' shop and cafe.* Continue past the car park and out along the surfaced road. This rises past a memorial woodland and offers spacious views over to the great mass of Dunsop and Croasdale Fells to the right.

Reaching the grandiose former reservoir keeper's house, take a stile in the corner and follow a track running beneath the grassy embankment of the dam. *Substantial waterworks buildings occupy the bowl below.* At the other end take a stile on the left and head away along an improving path. *This traces the line of the railway from Tosside.* It remains well above the shoreline and beneath a plantation, giving fine views over the broadening lake, with Whelp Stone Crag on the skyline above the vast Gisburn Forest.

When the trees end turn up the plantation side, briefly, then resume across a large rolling pasture to follow a better path which contours left to approach a plantation. A kissing-gate in a deer fence sends a clear path off through the trees. This soon emerges into better surrounds as a thoughtfully planted area is crossed to an identical gate back out. The damper path now runs on above a plantation to quickly emerge via a corner stile onto a road, with Stocks church just two minutes to the right.

St. James, Stocks-in-Bolland, was built in 1938 as a graveyard chapel where Stocks' souls had to be re-interred (just the dead ones - even water boards were never that vindictive). The old village church had itself only been built in 1852, and its stones went to the replacement. The route turns left along the road, through plantations and round to a causeway at the head of the reservoir, a good vantage point. Immediately across, a parallel path begins on the left and runs all the way back to the car park.

Winter at Stocks Reservoir

DUNSOP FELL

START *Slaidburn   Grid ref. SD 713523*

DISTANCE *8 miles (13km)*

ORDNANCE SURVEY MAPS
1:50,000
Landranger 103 - Blackburn & Burnley
1:25,000
Explorer OL41 - Forest of Bowland & Ribblesdale

ACCESS *Start from the village green. Car park across the road. Served by bus from Clitheroe and Settle.*

> *Rural walking to delectable sunken ways on easy fellsides before a lengthy return through unfrequented Croasdale*

   For a note on Slaidburn, please see page 18. Leave by the road past the Hark to Bounty, soon climbing steeply out of the village. *At the top this affords excellent views of the fell country ahead.* This road undulates for another mile or so, passing Ellerbeck Hall with its 1694 datestone. At a junction with Woodhouse Lane, note the old guidepost inscribed with the names Slaidburn and Hornby. *This is the old Hornby road with which you shall become better acquainted later in the walk.* Just a little further, over the brow and swinging left, take the first drive right, to Burnside Cottage.

   In these reedy pastures the drive crosses the line of the Roman road running north from Ribchester to Over Burrow in the Lune Valley. The former farmhouse at Burnside sits tucked under Dunsop Fell: without entering its grounds take a small gate to the right, over a plank bridge and up the enclosure side. Another gate, then a stile in a new section of wall see you emerge between tiny stream and wall into a large, reedy pasture. Continue ascending, soon crossing the stream and an initially moist, reedy way improves into a good path climbing to a gate at the top, onto the base of Dunsop Fell.

An inviting sunken way slants right towards the pronounced end of the spur. *Extensive views eastward include Easington Fell, the prow of Pendle Hill, Stocks Reservoir (better seen as height is gained) with Gisburn Forest behind.* Just short of the end of the spur double back with a choice of sunken ways, the main one being obvious. This classy staircase surmounts the full height of the spur above Dunsop Brook's deep enclave. *Looking back north Penyghent and Fountains Fell make shapely Yorkshire Dales skylines.*

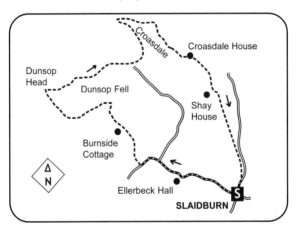

Bearing round to the right inside the shoulder, and now as good as level, the way crosses the beginnings of the brook and shortly falters at a brief but unmissable moist tract, best skirted to the right. By now the watershed wall appears ahead, and the path bears right to run parallel before finally joining it just short of a gate. *Views open out to reveal a moorland skyline that is the very heart of Bowland, with the dome of Totridge prominent to the south.* Here, at 1378ft/420m on Dunsop Head, is the walk's high point and also its turning point. *Paths up either spur of Dunsop Brook merge here, to go through the gate together to cross the heathery expanses into Whitendale.*

Don't pass through the gate, but double back right directly away from the wall, the thin path almost at once passing a modest scattering of stones. The next few minutes are moist underfoot, and though the path forges on through a potential swamp, easier ground is found by detouring round to the left, keeping just this side of a distinctive peaty section. Across the mire, the path effects a stunning transformation, heading confidently away over contrastingly dry, grassy fell. As descent commences it becomes part sunken. *Though a combination of bridleway usage and poor drainage downgrade this to a lesser standard than the ascent route, it nevertheless remains a smashing walk with time to appraise the distant panorama dominated by Three Peaks Country, with the much nearer Stocks Reservoir outspread ahead.* Joined by a wall as height is lost, it runs along to a corner to slant away again down to join the old Hornby Road. Here, just above the fell gate, it has lost its full surface and is concreted. *If tiring, this is the point to turn down for a quicker return.*

Your way goes left for a near-level walk during which time it swings left to head back for the wild fells. *Linking the Lune and Hodder Valleys, the Hornby Road - or Salters Way - has been a moorland highway for many centuries. It is best known as a salters' packway leading inland from Morecambe Bay to the farms of the Ribble Valley: the name Salter Fell, further west, recalls those days. For around three miles it overlays the Roman road crossed earlier in the walk. Around this bend the Roman's highway comes in, and together they are seen climbing past an old quarry high on Croasdale Fell: the wilds of Croasdale are now all yours. This classic crossing from Slaidburn to Hornby involves some 15 miles, though the largely hard surface makes it more suitable for biking than walking.*

During a slight descent (well short of New Bridge), turn off on a grassy path doubling sharply back down to the right. Zealously guided by marker posts, this is the old drive to the tumbledown House of Croasdale, which it suddenly reaches through a gate in a descending wall. *Possibly the site of a medieval hunting lodge, what was a ruin in the 1990s is now merely a pile of rubble.* Leaving it, a thin path slants down the moist, reedy pasture towards Croasdale Brook. Before reaching it the path turns right at a crumbling wall to run above it, commencing a lovely walk that parallels the gurgling stream. *Whilst a little waymarking is no bad thing, a valley full of yellow-topped posts detracts strongly from the untamed aspect of this lovely country.* When a wall crosses the beck a kissing-gate leads through it, and just a short way further downstream is a farm bridge. *Before crossing, note the tilted rock strata on the opposite bank.*

A rough track makes a steep ascent of the bank behind, affording a superb final view upstream before leaving you on a grassy brow, with Croasdale House appearing ahead. Descending towards it a track forms to cross a stream and runs along to the farm. Its drive leads out through the fields, but after crossing a tiny stream leave it and angle towards the brook to find a stile where wall and fence meet. Continue downstream to Shay House Farm, emerging via a stile onto its drive alongside a bridge.

Don't cross it, but take a wall-stile almost opposite. Turn downstream - noting the farming 'museum' on the opposite bank - but at the first bend as it swings away, keep straight on to a stile in the wall ahead. This final stage is a virtual bee-line for Slaidburn, as yet unseen. Head away to the far end, and from a wall-stile in the corner rise up the field with the scant remains of a line of stunted hawthorns. *Halt here to look back over a glorious scene beyond Shay House to the fells of your day's exertions.*

Maintain a straight line using stiles to pass through several fields: at one point there is a good view of Hammerton Hall back down to the left. Approaching a line of trees bear left to find a corner-stile into the edge of the trees. Go straight through and Slaidburn appears just ahead. Descend towards it, locating a stile back onto the road just short of the bridge over Croasdale Brook, which is crossed to enter the village.

Old guidepost,
Wood House Lane

3

EASINGTON FELL

START *Slaidburn   Grid ref. SD 713523*

DISTANCE *6^{1}2 miles (10^{1}2km)*

ORDNANCE SURVEY MAPS
1:50,000
Landranger 103 - Blackburn & Burnley
1:25,000
Explorer OL41 - Forest of Bowland & Ribblesdale

ACCESS *Start from the village green. Car park across the road.
Served by bus from Clitheroe and Settle.*

> *A brisk climb onto the fells between the Hodder and Ribble
> Valleys, with extensive panoramas into Bowland and Pendle*

To many people still a part of the traditional West Riding
of Yorkshire, Slaidburn remains the capital of Bowland, very much
as it has been since the days of the great hunting forest. The Hark
to Bounty pub was the home of the Forest courts, and the panelled
court room is preserved upstairs. The name dates back a century
to when a visiting squire discerned the sound of a distinguished
hound, causing him to exclaim 'Hark to Bounty'. The church of St
Andrew dates from the 15th century, and boasts a solid tower.
Inside are old box pews, a three-decker pulpit, and a Jacobean
rood screen. Adjacent is the old grammar school, founded in 1717,
a lovely building that survives today as the village school. A fine
war memorial stands in the village centre, which also boasts a Post
office/shop and youth hostel, once the Black Bull Inn. Overlooked
by the arched bridge is the spacious green, popular with visitors.
Alongside the car park a long established cafe does brisk trade,
while there is information and a tearoom at the Heritage Centre.

Leave by crossing the bridge and climb to the steep bend. Fifty yards beyond, a gate on the right sends an inviting fieldpath slanting away. *There are immediate views back over the village to the wall of fells beyond.* Approaching a wall, bear left with it on a good path running to a stile at the far end. Ahead is an early prospect of your fell for the day. Advance along the continuing wallside past a plantation. The brow reveals a fuller prospect of Easington Fell, and just beyond the end of the trees take a gate in the wall to resume on its other side. After a short descent to a road, cross straight over and down the drive to Broadhead Farm.

Pass left of the main buildings and leave round the back by crossing a farm bridge. Entering a scruffy arrangement of fenced enclosures, head half-right away to find a gate into the large, domed field, and head diagonally away to the far corner, with Skelshaw Brook just to the right. Continue down into the far corner where a stile is found, then ascend a field alongside newly planted trees. At the end drop down with the fence to cross the attractive Skelshaw Brook amid trees. From a small gate opposite ascend to a large

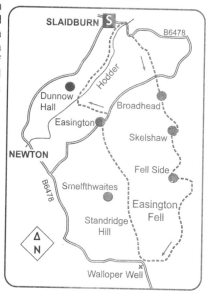

modern outbuilding, and follow the firm track on above a massive house at what was previously Skelshaw Farm. At the end another track is joined, turn sharply uphill on this to rise through the fields to the aptly-named Fell Side, tucked hard under the fell. *Look back to embrace an extensive panorama: in amongst the vastness of these eastern slopes - Totridge, Beatrix, Dunsop and Croasdale Fells - note also sleepy Newton nestling by the River Hodder.*

Enter the yard alongside kennels, and bear left behind the house to a gate onto the foot of the fell. A firm track heads away, quickly swinging up to the right to ascend above the side valley of Skelshaw Brook. A magnificent, sunken grassy way just a decade ago, the route has been trashed into just another rough track. *The views remain splendid, looking out from your own colourful fell to extensive Dales views from Fountains Fell along to Penyghent and Ingleborough.* As the gradients ease the track swings left above the upper reach of the brook, and finally returns to a more inviting condition throughout a leg-stretching tramp over Easington Fell. The infant beginnings of the brook are crossed as they emerge from a marshy hollow: later the way swings right up a gentle rake then on to the feeble cairn of Old Ned. *Note that if you wish to claim the true summit of Easington Fell, double back left across these gentle upper slopes to soon reach the small cairn at 1299ft/396m.*

The main route forges on across the moor. *Ahead, a working quarry is evident on the felltop: that, the mast above it and the presence of a road cruelly shatter any illusions of wilderness. Over to the left, as consolation, are the upper contours of Pendle Hill.* A similar grassy trackway merges from the left, and the way drops gently to approach the Clitheroe-Slaidburn road. Just before this point a green trod runs from a shooting butt to cross the grassy retaining wall of a former dam to meet the road a little higher, where spring water pours into stone troughs at Walloper Well. *The drained reservoir served a waterwheel that worked a small lead smelting mill downstream.*

Returning immediately to the moor, cross the tiny stream and - with no path - bear left, contouring around rough moorland in the company of telegraph poles. As these turn down to parallel the brook and the road, keep straight on over a little stream and along to an old stone shooting butt. While one sunken way descends straight from it, just a few yards above it are parallel sunken ways: these drop to cross a tiny sidestream then leave you free to ascend the easy slope to the prominent cairn on Standridge Hill just ahead. The cairn is made from a tiny scattering of rocks. This proves to be a broad felltop running north to Sadler Hill, with a pool sat in the saddle. Leave by resuming in the same direction on a faint trod to a well-defined edge. *Here take in a great prospect: below, fields fall to the Hodder, which winds between Newton and Slaidburn, with the great wall of Bowland fells as backdrop.* In the fields below is Smelfthwaites Farm: your way slants right down the bank to a tiny kink in the wall just below, which hides a stone stile.

Don't descend to the farm but slant across this reedy but after the initial steps, dry pasture to the isolated Padiham Barn in the far corner. From the stile alongside head down the fieldside, through several stiles, down a field centre to where an outer corner stile at the bottom continues down another fieldside. From a gate at the bottom alongside a triangular wood, a wall leads down to the farm buildings at Easington. *In this last field the big house in view across the river is the austere Victorian pile of Dunnow Hall.* Approaching Easington a track forms to cross a stream, becoming enclosed to emerge onto the narrow road.

Go right a few steps to a stile opposite. Head directly away, soon crossing the field centre and bearing gently left of a circular copse to find an iron kissing-gate hidden in a dip. Beneath it is an old iron footbridge, from where cross to the broad river bridge on the River Hodder just ahead. Across, ignore the track heading away towards the hall, and turn right on a permissive path upstream in glorious surrounds, a serene conclusion after the rigours of the fell. The grassy bank of the Hodder is a real delight, even allowing for the interruption of a sewage works where the path is deflected left, around three sides of it. *An impressive limestone scar thrusts out of the wooded bank above, while Slaidburn's church soon appears.* Back with the river, its bank is traced all the way back to the village. *Note the distinctive strip lynchets, ancient cultivation terraces, across two fields over to the left.* The way merges with a path from the church as it runs through trees to enter the green.

Walloper Well

HODDER BANK FELL

START *Newton*   *Grid ref. SD 697504*

DISTANCE *6$\frac{1}{2}$ miles (10$\frac{1}{2}$km)*

ORDNANCE SURVEY MAPS
1:50,000
Landranger 103 - Blackburn & Burnley
1:25,000
Explorer OL41 - Forest of Bowland & Ribblesdale

ACCESS *Start from the village centre. Car park at the Slaidburn end of the village. Served by Clitheroe-Slaidburn-Settle bus.*

A low fell with excellent views sandwiched between entirely delightful valley walking, often on the banks of the Hodder

   Newton-in-Bowland is a lovely, mellow stone village, dividing loyalties between Bowland's dark moors and the sparkling Hodder. In a prominent location near the river is the Parkers Arms, of late Georgian origin. Across the road is the equally attractive hall, while throughout the village are many delightful old buildings, including Salisbury Hall overlooking one of the luxuriant greens.

   Leave by descending the short way to Newton Bridge on the Hodder, and immediately across take a kissing-gate on the right. Head down-river, not quite on the bank as you pass a fence corner to find a stile part way along it. The path then runs atop a grassy bank to join the river fully. This is a grand spot backed by the moorland wall of Totridge. After a short while, through another stile the river turns away, and here bear left up an obvious line to a stile in the fence ahead. Continue through two further fields aiming for a barn that appears ahead at Foulscales. Just to its left is a stile in the hedge onto a road. Turn briefly right, then right again along a broad driveway. Remain on this enclosed way through some typical parkland, and on opening out, ignore a branch left and continue down to reach stone-arched Giddy Bridge on Birkett Brook.

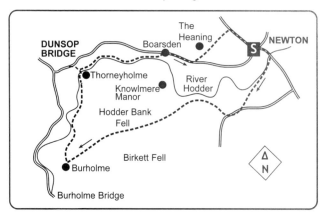

Across, leave the driveway and ascend the steep grassy bank to a stile above, at a distinct ditch. Victorian Knowlmere Manor, with its rare collection of chimneys, is seen through the trees. Rise again to a stile above, then slant right up the pasture to a stile in the fence part way up, well short of the barn at Matril Laithe. Rise more directly again now to a bridle-gate in the wall on the skyline above, between plantations. This accesses the open spaces of Hodder Bank Fell. *First, however, look back over an archetypal English landscape, true Hodder Country: Easington, Beatrix and Dunsop Fells, much rolling lower country, and on a clear day a fine array of Craven heights. Ahead, meanwhile, is just the moor: don't panic about the higher ground straight ahead though, that's Totridge across the other side of the valley!* A good path rises through the tussocks. To the left is the wooded top of Kitcham Hill, summit of Birkett Fell. The brow is quickly reached, marked by a stone post at the walk's high point a little over 656ft/200m. *Looking back, Penyghent joins Fountains Fell on the Dales skyline.*

Though occasionally moist, the path runs grandly on before dropping gently to a corner of the fell. From the stile in this wall corner a fine path escapes a moist corner and heads away, dropping down by a fence on the edge of Fielding Clough, through bracken. This remains a grand descent throughout its course, with super views of the valley to come, and Burholme Bridge appearing beneath the limestone skyline of Long Knots. At the bottom a stile finally crosses the fence, then drop down the field bottom to a stile just above the stream, then down again the short way to a foot-bridge accessing Burholme Farm. *Centuries ago this was a hamlet, and excavations have revealed much evidence of busier times.*

Don't use the bridge but take the track off to the right, fading but crossing a couple of fields to gain the Hodder with Langden Holme Farm just across. *From these fields look back to a skyline broken by the limestone knolls that enrich this corner of Bowland.* Upstream a rough pasture with odd trees is entered via an old iron gate. The gentle watersmeet of Langden Brook and the river is passed, with shapely Langden Bridge seen marking the brook's final crossing. Shortly a substantial iron aqueduct is reached. *Erected by Blackburn Corporation Waterworks in 1882 to carry a pipeline to their thirsty townsfolk, it is fronted by an antiquated turnstile which gives access to a better vantage point over the Hodder.*

Continue along your bank through a couple more stiles, before a tree-lined pasture leads to a farm drive at Thorneyholme. *Once owned by the Towneley family, the hall has since been a nunnery, hotel and health farm.* The path is ushered round the outside of the house to its access bridge, to enjoy a second watersmeet as the short-lived River Dunsop is absorbed by the Hodder in a delectable setting. The bridge carries the drive, and thus your path, out to emerge into Dunsop Bridge opposite the car park.

Dunsop Bridge is a tiny Bowland village, under the influence of the Duchy of Lancaster estate and the water company. Before leaving, have a look at the phone box, the 100,000th public pay-phone installed by BT. This claims to mark the centre of Great Britain and 401 associated islands, having been calculated by the Ordnance Survey to a 10-figure grid reference. Town names adorn the windows, while outside, in a little rock garden, wooden posts mark points of the compass. More regular features near the duck-patrolled riverside green are St George's church, a trout farm, garage, Post office/shop/tearoom and WC.

Leave by returning to the bridge on the Hodder. Don't cross, but take an iron kissing-gate on the left to head upstream. At the end pass through a small wooded corner before resuming with the river. Simply ramble along the riverbank, passing a surprisingly incongruous aqueduct bridge on the river. On again, you reach the inflowing Rough Syke. Turn upstream a few paces to a footbridge on it, followed by a stile and then downstream with this beck the short way back to the Hodder. Here stands an alarmingly perilous suspension footbridge you might be grateful isn't on your route!

Resume upstream to a gate through which a grassy track forms. This quickly leaves the river to slant gently up the field to the far corner. Don't pass along the front of the cottage, but take a tiny gate to its left, and up the side to a gate onto the road at Boarsden. Turn right along here for ten minutes or so until a stile on the left. Rise up the field to the trees ahead, finding a stile in their midst, as an old driveway comes in on the right. Head away from the stile, with a pond at the isolated house of Heaning over the hedge to your left.

At the end cross the modern drive to a stile in the corner, then ascend an unexpectedly moist bank (a tilted bog) to dry ground above. Continue rising with a line of trees to a wall-stile. Just above is the brow, over which advance to a gap-stile just right of the corner, marked by a massive standing stone. Continue to a stile at the end which deposits you onto a back road. Turn right down this lane into the edge of Newton, passing on the brow the Quaker burial ground, while lower down is the old Friends' Meeting House. *Dating from the 1760s, it only ceased its original role in 1988 to become a private house.*

Friends' Meeting House, Newton

5

WHITEWELL GORGE

START Whitewell   Grid ref. SD 659468

DISTANCE 7¹4 miles (11¹2km)

ORDNANCE SURVEY MAPS
1:50,000
Landranger 102 - Preston & Blackpool **or**
Landranger 103 - Blackburn & Burnley
1:25,000
Explorer OL41 - Forest of Bowland & Ribblesdale

ACCESS Start from the centre of the hamlet. Roadside parking, and a small car park by the church. Served by Clitheroe-Slaidburn-Settle bus. An alternative start is Burholme Bridge.

Magnificent panoramas and limestone features above the richly wooded gorge of the Hodder at lovely Whitewell

Cheek by jowl at Whitewell are pub and church - indeed there is not a great deal else, but it's a charming spot. The little church of St Michael dates from 1818, on the site of a much earlier chapel. The Inn at Whitewell is an old fashioned country hotel: pay extra for a peat fire in your room! This was the former manor house, and incorporated in the present building are parts dating back 500 years. The inside of the place lives up to its attractive exterior, and welcoming rooms exude the right atmosphere.

Leave by the minor road climbing from the green and bound for Clitheroe, past the small social hall. Just beyond a driveway turn up a few steps to a gate, from which a path rises to the house above. Turn right in front of it, and a grassy track heads past an aqueduct installation and slowly slants up past a small old quarry to the top corner of the field. *Already you enjoy glorious views, across to Totridge and back up-dale to the fells of the Dunsop Valley.* From the gate at the top ignore the fading track, and turn right along the wall-top to tall iron gates in the corner. The way now simply traces the adjacent fence on an easy contour through several lush pastures. *Throughout this stage savour views over the wooded Whitewell Gorge to limestone knolls beneath the high moorland wall of Fair Oak Fell, while Longridge Fell forms the flat skyline directly ahead.* Passing a small quarry with intriguing tilted rocks, the fence finally ends at identical iron gates. Keep straight on, bearing right to pass through a gate at the far corner and advance a little further to a gate onto the road.

Follow this briefly past the trees and escape at a stile on the right. Head diagonally away down a vast pasture, lower down bearing right to where the trees protrude. Pass down their side to a stile at the bottom, and keep on along a distinct bank well above the river. Swinging left a green track forms, and drops steadily towards a tree-lined sidestream which is forded close to the riverbank. From a kissing-gate just beyond advance to old gateposts, then slightly up and along to a stile behind. Now cross to a tree-lined stream, and slant up the bank well left of the trees ahead, to a stile onto the bend of a farm road. Turn right here, dropping down to the river-bank to approach the farm at Stakes.

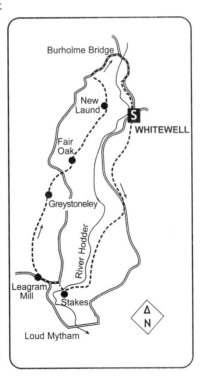

27

This fine old house dates from the 17th century and features mullioned and transomed windows: a tablet above the nearer door bears a Latin inscription. On your right is the river crossing of Stakes Hippins, a sturdy set of 30 stones that would only be deemed impassable in times of flood. *In this case you would have to retrace the farm drive to cross the river at Doeford Bridge, downstream.* This is the turning point of the walk, and a grand place to linger. So cross the Hodder in style, and from a stile behind cross the field to a farm bridge in front of the house at Wardsley.

Joining a back road turn left, climbing to a T-junction. Keep right, rising to the environs of Leagram Mill. Before the first house (Leagram Mill Barn) turn right up a firm driveway which shortly rises up a fieldside to a junction by the limestone knolls of Knot Hill. Advance past the residential conversion of Knot Barn and along to Lower Greystoneley. Keep on past the house to pass between ramshackle barns to a gate into the trees. A more inviting cart track drops down to a concrete ford and footbridge, then ascends back out to run as a pleasant green way to Higher Greystoneley. *With its 1873 datestone this former farmhouse is now surrounded by modern housing.* Pass through them, and at the start of the drive take a stile on the right to cross the reedy field to a stile onto a back road. Cross straight over to another stile just ahead, then bear right to the cluster of barns at Fair Oak.

Pass round the right side of the large, sturdy stone barn. *Locally known as the Gunnary, it bears a 1729 datestone and sports a whole range of slit windows.* Through the yard, a junction of ways is reached at the centre. Turn left on a drive past the house, but before the second house turn right down a rough track. *The higher house is the old coach house, sporting mullioned windows and a tablet on the side proclaiming 'John Parkinson Dorothy his wife and Thomas his son 1716'.* The track drops to a gate and then runs on a fieldside directly away, with the limestone knoll of New Laund Hill ahead and the Whitewell Gorge down to the right. At the end take a stile on the right and follow the curving fence away, reaching a ladder-stile in the limestone wall ahead.

A faint path heads away, with the broader option crossing a shoulder of the high knoll while a thinner path contours right. *Either way you will savour a super revelation of Hodder Country at its finest. Behind, the Whitewell Gorge ushers the river down through rich woodland carpeted with springtime bluebells, backed by Longridge Fell. Ahead, the prospect up-dale embraces Totridge, Mellor Knoll, Staple Oak Fell, the Dunsop Valley, Middle Knoll, Beatrix Fell, Dunsop Fell, Burholme Bridge and Hodder Bank Fell.*

Part way down the other side pass through a gate in a fence, and by a fence corner beneath an old quarry a track forms to descend into the farmyard at New Laund. *A forest keepers' house once existed here. Hidden in the woods close by is the 65ft long cave of Fairy Holes, which has revealed animal bones and an Early Bronze Age urn.* Turn left along the drive out, passing an old farm cheese press used up to the 1860s. The drive runs out onto a road, where turn right to descend to a junction at Burholme Bridge.

Having lingered over the bridge's two irregular arches and savoured fine views both up and down the valley, turn right downstream with the Hodder, where oystercatchers stalk the banks. Part way along, a stile in the hedge on the right sends a thoughtfully provided concession path into the field to escape the tarmac by paralleling the road to Whitewell. At the end a wooded bank and a lovely river bend form a classic Bowland scene looking across to Totridge. The path crosses a footbridge on a sidestream and runs through woodland to emerge alongside the hotel.

Burholme Bridge

29

6

BRENNAND VALLEY

START *Dunsop Bridge*   *Grid ref. SD 660500*

DISTANCE *8¹4 miles (13km)*

ORDNANCE SURVEY MAPS
1:50,000
Landranger 102 - Preston & Blackpool **or**
Landranger 103 - Blackburn & Burnley
1:25,000
Explorer OL41 - Forest of Bowland & Ribblesdale

ACCESS *Start from the village centre. Car park. Served by Clitheroe-Slaidburn-Settle bus.*

> *A super walk linking two contrasting side valleys of the Hodder by a memorable crossing of Whin Fell*

         For a note on Dunsop Bridge, please see page 24. Cross the bridge by the Post office and follow the road away past the war memorial. At a junction with the Lancaster road turn right for the Trough. *The modern guidepost supplements a far more individual one dated 1739, with mileage for Slaidburn, Hornby, 'Clithero' and 'Lankster'. An old iron post embedded in the top forlornly points to the 'Trough road'.* On past the school, the isolated Roman Catholic church is reached. *Our Lady & St Hubert's dates from 1864, and with some nice stained glass, it has links with the Towneley family. St Hubert, incidentally, died in 727, and was a patron saint of hunters and protector against mad dogs. You shouldn't need his services on this walk.*
    Striding out, a cattle-grid is crossed and the road runs free through glorious surrounds. *The bulky wall on the skyline to the left is Totridge.* Shortly, turn down a drive to a bridge on Langden

Brook, and follow the drive just a short way to where a stile sends a concession path into the field on the right. A bridge crosses Hareden Brook to swing right to a stile by Langden Brook. Head upstream, initially flanked by a wall before meeting a stile in a fence. *Conspicuous up on the road are Smelt Mill Cottages, base of the Bowland Pennine Mountain Rescue Team. Here was a smelt mill for lead mined a mile further up the road, which you shall shortly be passing.* The inviting grassy sward leads to a substantial bridge. Cross it to gain the broad Langden drive through pine trees, and turn right to return to the road.

Continuing, the road becomes briefly enclosed to pass through Sykes Farm. *This centuries-old settlement was once a vaccary farm and a sizeable farming hamlet - indeed there are still three habitations here today.* Beyond Sykes, the road starts to run more freely through increasingly encroaching steep fellsides. *This little side valley leading through the Trough of Bowland is known as Losterdale, and* its stream is a tinkling delight when not under contract to the water company.

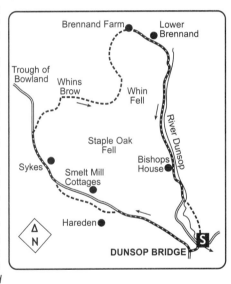

Just past the farm mixed woodland on the right shelters an old quarry, its contorted strata evident to all. Another quarry is soon located on the left also, above a well-preserved limekiln. Just after the road bridges the beck, Trough Barn is reached: this is a good time to leave as the road begins its haul to the Grey Stone of Trough, the traditional county boundary.

Through the gate a distinct track climbs above a wooded bank, deflected left outside a plantation to a stile at the top. Here the original sunken way is paralleled by a track to the right, merging as the going eases out to run to the top end of a small wood. Through the stile are the sorry remains of Trough House. Just beyond, the track rises right with a wall. Ahead is a broad amphitheatre below the skyline horseshoe of Whins Brow and Staple Oak Fell. Curving uphill the track passes through a stile in the wall, and runs on between a small wood and a wall, briefly, before opening out into rougher terrain. As the wall drops away a little further along, a thinner path takes over. This maintains a clear course as it slants ever gradually up through reeds to the top corner, and a bridle-gate in the wall. Entering open moorland a grand little path climbs away, briefly steeply alongside a ravine. The path quickly breasts the level ground of the moortop, where Whins Brow and Staple Oak Fell meet, and civilisation seems comfortingly distant. *Vast swathes of Bowland moors are revealed, whilst you can also look out to Winter Hill, Pendle Hill and Waddington Fell.*

Joining a fence from the right the path runs to a watershed fence junction, and the only moist moment of the walk. At 1410ft/430m, this is also the walk's high point. Over the stile/gate head straight on through heathery terrain, quickly swinging left to find the ground falling away suddenly to reveal a cracking prospect of the Brennand Valley at your feet, immersed in sombre moorland.

Find a heathery couch just off the path, and savour the moment. Your objective of Brennand Farm is directly below, its few green pastures couched in a moorland bowl running from Ward's Stone to Wolfhole Crag. The low col behind the farm was the site of a lead mine - this ore was also carried over Ouster Rake to the smelt mill.

Old guidepost, Dunsop Bridge

The next stage is an absorbing few minutes as the path descends Ouster Rake, which in extremely unlikely severe wintry conditions might initially demand a little care.

The slanting descent may be a bridleway on the map, but today it is very much a footpath on the ground. The Brennand Stones across to the left form a colourful amphitheatre. The most enjoyable part is soon over as you drop to a gate in a wall-corner. Beyond it a thinner path heads away before turning to descend to a gate at the bottom. From here continue straight down a larger pasture to the waiting Brennand Farm. A couple of small enclosures lead to the yard at the rear, and behind the house its surfaced drive heads off down-dale.

Whilst the return is largely on surfaced road, it has virtually no vehicles, many good verges, and grand surroundings. A bridge over the River Brennand leads to Low Brennand Farm. Rising away, a dark wall of conifers in the main valley awaits, and a junction is quickly reached with a long view down-valley. *The left branch runs up Whitendale to the similarly isolated Whitendale Farm. These valleys were devastated by floods after a freak cloudburst in 1967.* After looking back to a fine Brennand scene, turn down to the right, the road leading unfailingly back to the village.

Winding down to an information panel by a footbridge, the confluence of Brennand and Whitendale rivers is reached. Here the River Dunsop is born, destined for a meagre two miles of existence before entering the Hodder at Dunsop Bridge. The road crosses the former and past unsightly waterworks, beyond which note the dry course of the old river. From here the way is channelled too, by plantations on the lower flanks of Staple Oak and Beatrix Fells. Enclosure is never claustrophobic, however, and more breathing space is granted as the road runs to the solitary Bishops House. An open half-mile beside the river leads to a footbridge on it. Cross to a woodland path downstream to a terrace of stone dwellings at Holme Head. The drive leads back, sometimes with the winding river, to emerge by the Post office.

Roadsign limekiln above Sykes Farm

33

FIENDSDALE

START *Langden Intake*   *Grid ref. SD 632511*

DISTANCE *9^{1}2 miles (15km)*

ORDNANCE SURVEY MAPS
1:50,000
Landranger 102 - Preston & Blackpool
1:25,000
Explorer OL41 - Forest of Bowland & Ribblesdale

ACCESS *Start from a parking area at the start of Langden Intake water company road, on the Trough road two miles west of Dunsop Bridge.* • *OPEN ACCESS - see page 9.*

> *An excursion into the Langden Valley seeks out deep recesses in the folds of the hills, linked by a high level moorland trek*

From the gates head along the surfaced drive flanked by pines. Visible over to the right is Sykes Farm, the last settlement this side of the Trough. At Langden House the drive bears round to the right, quickly ending at the intake works. Beyond a gate a rough track sets out into the lonely valley of Langden Brook. *There's a strong hint of Scotland here, suggesting a long walk-in to higher country as yet hidden behind foothills.*

A spell by the level flood plain and beck is bettered as the rough track makes a brief, steep climb above a tiny wooded bank: on leveling out it forks, keep left on the level one. Easy walking on a level terrace allows time to become acquainted with this lovely dale. Grand views are enjoyed throughout, with Fiendsdale's upper recesses appearing far ahead: part way along you pass beneath a hardy, stunted oakwood. After minor undulations, a rise to a junction can be eschewed where a small cairn indicates a footpath that maintains the contouring line. Just ahead, the roof of Langden Castle appears, and the path rejoins the track to descend to it. *The 'castle' is something of a disappointment, being merely a stone built shooters' or shepherd's lodge and shelter. The grassy sward at the front is a good place to sit and take it all in, looking directly into the substantial side valley of Bleadale. This should not be confused with Bleasdale, to the south over the main watershed.*

From the front of the building, head away through a defence of reeds to ford Langden Brook above its confluence with Bleadale Water. The latter is less easy to cross, do this after the fence on your left has first accomplished the task. Just a little further, take a gate in the fence, and a path becomes clear as it surmounts a small bank and forges on to penetrate this very beautiful clough. *This way would appear to*

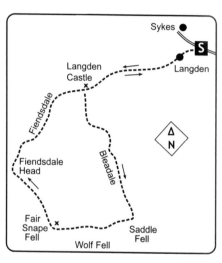

have been inadvertently omitted from the definitive map, as a number of decades ago, Lancashire expert Jessica Lofthouse described it as a centuries-old track, at that time still used by local farmers as a short-cut to the Trough and Wyresdale.

Though the fence flits about with the brook, simply remain on this eastern bank. As the valley briefly narrows, the fence returns to be crossed at a gate: the path runs between heathery walls before the valley re-opens and you emerge via another gate onto a sweeping bend. As a sidestream falls towards you, don't be tempted by the shooters' path rising distinctly up the flank to the left. Turn right with the fence, which turns back over the brook and departs, leaving you alone in the magnificent upper confines of Bleadale.

The thin path crosses the sidestream, and on a further five level minutes to a confluence. Here twin stream merge, and though Brown Berry Clough to the right is more pronounced, remain on the bank of the left branch. Continue upstream with a final cluster of trees opposite. At once far more confined, scale the initially steep bank, and the slim path picks up above a few trees on your own side. *This delicate path would not take kindly to accommodating large groups, but who would want to be in this delightful spot amid an army of ramblers?* The final stage is a distinct trod through thick heather: pause to look back over an array of interlocking spurs folding back towards the moors beyond Langden Brook.

A confluence with a little fall is passed before finally gaining an amphitheatre where tiny streamlets form Bleadale Water. In this heathery bowl you might be anywhere, the view in these upper reaches being only of your enclosing moors. The thin path shadows the right-most streamlet, playfully re-crossing every few steps as you emerge onto the open moor. The path then simply forges south-westwards through gently rising heather, aided by the odd marker post as the watershed fence appears ahead. Reaching it within ten minutes or so, turn right and shadow it past a pool, the thin trod being less help than the fence's presence. *Looking around, distant views are now on offer, the sweeping moorland skyline of Bowland - with the crest of Totridge particularly prominent back along the ridge - is added to by Longridge Fell to the south, backed by the West Pennine Moors, and Pendle Hill further back to the left.*

A junction with a fence rising from Saddle Fell is quickly reached, and here take a stile to resume on the south side of the watershed fence. This move is proven worthwhile when joined by a path crossing from a ladder-stile in the other fence. This good path runs over improving ground, noting as you go one of a series of numbered boundary stones, this being '30'. *All bear the lettering 'WD' (War Department), a reference to the area's former use for military training.* A gentle rise leads past the prone '29'. *Views ahead open out to reveal a wide seascape, while over to the left the rounded top of Parlick can be discerned.* At the next fence corner you reach Fair Snape Fell. A further arrangement of stile and stone '28' mark the walk's summit. The cairn just to the right stands at 1706ft/520m, though its lower top at 1673ft/510m across the marshy plateau is more often visited (see WALK 11).

A step-stile gives access to the summit cairn, and it is this fence that gives a long, easy descent north-west to Fiendsdale Head. Again, either side of the fence might be followed, though the south side is probably preferable. The first section is entirely delightful on short-cropped turf between peaty knolls. Enjoy it, for soon moist ground takes over for the rest of the way down to the saddle. Across Fiendsdale Head rise the heathery Bleasdale Moors. At a padlocked gate look back to the shapelier edge of Fair Snape, and across Bleasdale to the colourful crest of diminutive Beacon Fell. Beyond the gate a slight rise leads to a stile and notice just prior to a fence corner. If still on the south side, cross the stile and head north on an initially messy path with the fence parallel over to the left. This is the Bleasdale-Fiendsdale right of way.

Within a minute the way improves, a peaty channel leading the path to easier ground. The head of Fiendsdale quickly forms, and a solid path takes over in the heather. This remains a brilliant path, soon visible some way hence as it contours around heathery flanks. The return to the valley floor comes suddenly in the form of a rapid descent of Fiendsdale Nab. The dale is gained at the confluence of Langden Brook and Fiendsdale Water, a grand spot for a break. Only the former brook is crossed, which should be easy if Bleadale Water was managed earlier in the walk. With the valley floor dead flat, the path gains a modest bank and runs on to return to Langden Castle, merging into the shooters' track for the final yards. All that remains is to retrace steps back to the start.

Langden Castle

TOTRIDGE

START *Dunsop Bridge*   Grid ref. *SD 660500*

DISTANCE *7¹2 miles (12km)*

ORDNANCE SURVEY MAPS
1:50,000
Landranger 102 - Preston & Blackpool **or**
Landranger 103 - Blackburn & Burnley
1:25,000
Explorer OL41 - Forest of Bowland & Ribblesdale

ACCESS *Start from the village green. Car park. Served by Clitheroe-Slaidburn-Settle bus. • OPEN ACCESS - see page 9.*

A steep but memorable climb to a prominent Bowland landmark, with a rougher descent to a lonely valley

For a note on Dunsop Bridge, see page 24. Cross the bridge by the Post office to leave the green and follow the road away past the war memorial. At a junction turn right for the Trough, on the Lancaster road. *The modern guidepost supplements a far more individual one dated 1739, and inscribed with mileage for Hornby, Slaidburn, 'Clithero' and 'Lankster'. An old iron post embedded in the top forlornly points to the 'Trough road'.* On past the primary school is the isolated Roman Catholic church of Our Lady & St Hubert. *Dating from 1864, and with some nice stained glass, it has links with the Towneley family. St Hubert, incidentally, died in 727, a patron saint of hunters and protector against mad dogs.*

Striding out, a cattle-grid is crossed and the road runs free through glorious surrounds. The bulky wall of Totridge is prominent up to the left, awaiting your feet. Shortly a drive goes down left to a bridge over Langden Brook. Cross it and follow the drive along to the farming hamlet of Hareden. Cross the bridge on Hareden Brook to run along the characterful front of the farmhouse (1656 date-stone), then quickly back over another bridge before an attractive cottage. At once leave the track by a stile on the left to rise up the field, pausing to look back over this sequestered scene.

Bear left to a stile and gate at the top corner to meet a track, which skirts the outside of a plantation before rapidly fading. Simply climb half-right up the steep, expansive green pasture, eventually meeting up with a wall near the top. Go left with it and a green track soon forms to approach the top corner. Up to the right is the seamed face of Totridge, while behind is an intimate prospect of the fair Trough of Bowland. Before the top, however, get close to the wall so as not to miss the gate/stile from where a concession path sets off (around 150 yards before the top corner). Entering a vast sloping rough pasture, curve round beneath the top wall to the far corner.

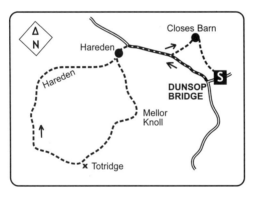

A fence takes over to resume the ascent, to a stile at the top onto the open fellside. Continue the steep climb, now with a wall again and a thin path forming on delectable turf. *Down to the left is the Hodder curving beneath Hodder Bank Fell overtopped by Pendle Hill; better still is the prospect of Hareden Farm below you, backed by rolling moorland spurs leading to the Trough.* Higher, as the wall angles away left, simply continue straight up the path which suddenly meets a hugely inviting grassy rake. This stunning old path slants left then right through bilberries to fade at the edge of the climb. A thinner path takes up the running again, rising gently left onto the heathery moortop. As this fades it runs onto the broad ridge straight ahead, at which point swing left for the final minutes: the Ordnance Survey column soon appears, and a thin trod is likely to be found leading past a tiny pool couched in heather to gain the trig point surmounting a little peat bank.

At 1627ft/496m Totridge is one of the great Bowland's landmarks. Local colleagues in view include Parlick, Fair Snape Fell, Ward's Stone, Wolfhole Crag and White Hill. Further north, Penyghent is a shapely representative of Three Peaks Country. Your objective now is the valley of Hareden Brook, currently unseen to the west. So, without a path for the next half-hour, simply head down the opposite side of the fell to the one you ascended, and watch where you put your feet: poor visibility need not deter you, there's little scope for going wrong. Through heather and occasional peat the descent gently begins, and very quickly you will see a scarred shooters' track zigzagging up past a high-level cabin on the flank of Hareden Fell opposite. It matters little as to where you reach the valley, but aim right of the zigzags in order to meet that track on the valley floor. Grass gradually starts to replace heather, and you can pick your spot as to where the brook is crossed to join the firm track. Should you encounter a fenced enclosure lower down, then simply deflect around it to the right.

Once on the track, all that remains is to follow it downstream through this attractive valley. Another cabin stands below the track, which after a little kink drops onto the flats to shadow the lively brook. This highly enjoyable conclusion runs to a footbridge and ford at the limit of open country. Remain on the track (concession path) as it runs by water intakes to the house ahead, whereupon it becomes surfaced to lead back out through Hareden onto the road.

To vary the finish, after passing back over the cattle-grid, take an early gate on the left and slant up the large pasture a little before contouring across it, part way on aiming for the house at Closes Barn ahead. Towards the end a wall corner is passed to send you on to the very corner. Through the stile advance on above the cottages to join the Dunsop Valley access road. Turn right on this, through a field to a fork by Forestry Commission cabins, where keep left to run back out into the village, re-crossing the Dunsop.

LITTLE BOWLAND

START *Chipping   Grid ref. SD 622432*

DISTANCE *7¹4 miles (11¹2km)*

ORDNANCE SURVEY MAPS
1:50,000
Landranger 102 - Preston & Blackpool **or**
Landranger 103 - Blackburn & Burnley
1:25,000
Explorer OL41 - Forest of Bowland & Ribblesdale

ACCESS *Start from the village centre. Car parks. Served by Clitheroe-Longridge-Preston bus.*

A leisurely ramble around the pastoral farming area known as Little Bowland, between Chipping and the River Hodder

For a note on Chipping, please see page 44. Leave by the side road heading away past the church, and at a junction fork right to descend by a factory. *This celebrated chairmaker's dates from the 1840s and is a local institution.* Climb past it to a lovely millpond that once powered it. Part way along turn off at a stile by a drive, and head up the fieldside. *Ahead, Parlick thrusts itself forward, while looking back, Longridge Fell forms a long skyline over the village, with Pendle Hill further back to its left.* Keep straight on at the top, and from a stile at the end advance across a large field, bearing left to the bank above Dobson's Brook. A little further, pass beneath a small hollow, and an improving little path heads off to contour around the bank to a stile part way down. From it the thin path runs on to enter scattered trees and reach a footbridge over the right arm of a confluence. Climb the field behind to the left of the house at Windy Hills, and turn right into the yard.

Leave up the far side of the barn, where a green track climbs the fieldside. Through a gate at the top it swings right and peters out, simply remain with the fence on your right through several stiles. A wall takes over, and just before a modest brow, a waymark sends you off to the left, crossing to a stile then bearing right to a corner stile onto the farm road to Burnslack (not quite as per map). Instead of following the road up, turn sharp right along another track, an old road. *On the brow it reveals a good view out to the twosome of Pendle Hill and Longridge Fell, while Burnslack and Fair Oak Fells form a great wall above you, joined by Totridge.* The track enters rough pasture at a gate to ford Leagram Brook, with stepping-stones also here. At the end you are on the walk's modest high point at around 780ft/238m, greeted by a view of the ridge of Long Knots, the brink of limestone country. A long descent through a reedy enclosure leads to the farm at Lickhurst.

Without entering the farm complex, go steeply left down the access road. Before the road bridge, instead take a footbridge at a confluence. Climb the field to a stile and up again, well left of a small old limestone quarry, and on to a gate. Now bear left around the field-edge, with Dinkling Green appearing ahead. Remain on the boundary, pass-

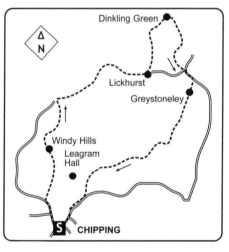

ing a small pool and at the corner pass through a gate and turn sharp right down the fenceside. A gate in a damp corner below transfers you back across the fence, to advance towards the farm. Nearer, a track forms, going through a gate and beneath a small plantation to enter the farmyard. *Dinkling Green is a settlement of some age, having once been a much busier hamlet and still boasting a fine collection of old barns.*

Go straight ahead to leave by the drive. *Passing over the brook and then a cattle-grid, look back to see the splendid frontage of the 17th century Eshenoke House, with its mullioned windows.* The drive curves round to the right under Long Knots. *This is a grand promenade, looking across to the high moorland wall of Fair Oak Fell to Totridge, while ahead is the long skyline of aptly named Longridge Fell.* Remain on the drive which curves round again beneath the knoll to emerge onto a junction of back roads, and a plethora of signage. Alongside stands a surviving red telephone box. Advance straight on, briefly, just as far as a drive on the right. Turn along this to Higher Greystoneley. With its 1873 datestone, this former farmhouse is now surrounded by modern housing.

Pass straight on between the buildings, continuing away on an inviting, enclosed grassy way. The track descends to a ford and footbridge in the wood, then climbs to Lower Greystoneley. Again forge straight on, its drive running to Knot Barn, another recent conversion to a dwelling in front of the broken skyline of Knot Hill. Turn up to the right here, a green track running between a pond and a limekiln. Ignore the track's turn to the right, and keep on past a substantial old limestone quarry. At the end, bear gently left to locate a stile in the fence ahead. From it bear left down the wooded bank, a grassy spur swinging back right down to reach a footbridge for a second crossing of Leagram Brook, a grand spot.

Slant right up the opposite bank to a stile, quickly levelling out into a large, reedy pasture. Now march straight on with a fence on the right, enjoying a moorland skyline above, with the long wall of Longridge across the Vale of Loud. After several intervening stiles the fence finally ends, but keep straight on through the parkland of Leagram Hall to join the drive. *Leagram Hall is on the site of a lodge in this former deer park, and with its long-standing Catholic connections was a 16th century refuge for priests.* Follow the drive down to the road, and on joining it take advantage of a concession bridleway which runs through the belt of trees, shadowing the road until joining it further along at an attractive lodge. Chipping church tower is a magnet now. Arriving at the war memorial, turn right for the village centre, passing the old watermill (the wheel might be glimpsed through foliage) on Chipping Brook to finish.

CHIPPING FELLS

START *Chipping   Grid ref. SD 622432*

DISTANCE *7¹⁄2 miles (12km)*

ORDNANCE SURVEY MAPS
1:50,000
Landranger 102 - Preston & Blackpool
1:25,000
Explorer OL41 - Forest of Bowland & Ribblesdale

ACCESS *Start from the village centre. Car parks. Served by Clitheroe-Longridge-Preston bus. • OPEN ACCESS - see page 9.*

> *A moderately wild walk on the delightful fells rising behind Chipping. Almost entirely excellent underfoot; classic views*

Chipping is an attractive village whose origins pre-date its emergence as a market town in 1203. Features of interest include two pubs, a cafe, Post office and couple of shops, all near the junction of the two principal streets. Worth seeing is a former school, endowed by cloth merchant John Brabin in 1683. It sports mullioned windows, and forms a tidy group with adjacent almshouses. St Bartholomew's church has 16th century origins: great semi-circular steps from the main street are a novel feature. Wolfen Mill dairy produces high quality Lancashire cheeses.

Leave by a side road heading away between church and cafe. At a junction on the edge of the village fork right, descending to Chipping's celebrated chairmakers. Climb past it to the lovely mill pond that once provided its power. Part way along it turn off at a stile by a drive, and head up the right side of the field. *Parlick thrusts itself forward in readiness, while Longridge Fell forms a long skyline back over the village, with Pendle Hill set further back.* Keep straight on at the top: ahead now is the great cirque of fells that is to be yours. From a stile at the end, advance across a large field, bearing left to the bank of Dobson's Brook.

A little further, at a small, reedy hollow, an improving path heads off to contour around the bank to a stile. From it the path runs on to enter scattered trees and reach a footbridge over the right arm of a confluence. Climb the field behind to the left of the house at Windy Hills, and follow its rough drive over Dobson's Brook up onto a road. *Note, just before the road, an attractive little pond.* Cross straight over and up the drive to aptly-named Saddle End Farm. *The cone of Parlick now dominates the scene in style.*

Rise into the yard and up a grassy track climbing directly away. This runs through a couple of enclosures past a small plantation, then rises as braided ways to a ladder-stile onto the fell. The good track continues, working a smashing way up onto the grassy spur of Saddle Fell. As the ways split again, cairns suggest the middle one, though any is worthy. *Looking back, Pendle and Longridge front a massive line of South*

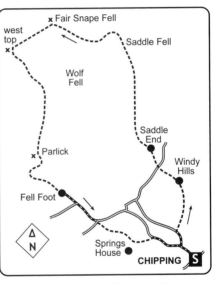

and West Pennines, while Parlick starts to lose dominance. A prominent cairn with stake precedes arrival at a low ruin, as grassiness gives way to rougher ground including heather. Nearing a fence rising with the head of the brook on the left, remain on the track which peters out just as a stile is reached.

Crossing to Wolf Fell, a thin path heads away past shooting butts, a delightful way rising imperceptibly through the heather. *A glimpse of Parlick reveals only its upper reaches now, though before going too far, turn to look back over a moorland foreground to a prospect of Three Peaks Country.* The path expires at a path junction in front of a fence: turn right the few steps to a fence junction on Fair Snape Fell's true summit. A ladder-stile carries you over the fence, though another stile invites a short detour to the sturdy summit cairn at 1706ft/520m. *Also by the fence junction is a prostrate boundary stone. The lettering 'WD' (War Department), is a reference to the area's former usage for military training. The prospect is outstanding, with Three Peaks Country being joined by Morecambe Bay and the Lakeland Fells beyond a sprawl of Bowland.*

Back at the fence-corner, head south with the fence just as far as an intervening stile, from where bear right for the short stroll to the waiting cairns on Fair Snape's more popular western top, at 1673ft/510m. *This is very much a place to linger, as cairns and an Ordnance Survey column play second fiddle to a practical stone shelter. Paddy's Pole, as marked on maps, is only intermittently embedded in the sprawling cairn that bears the name.* Leave by striking south-east for Parlick, a delightful short-cropped path crossing an intervening fence-stile to regain the descending ridge. *The fields and farms of Bleasdale are encircled far below: beyond this neatly packaged farmland, the island-like Beacon Fell appears profoundly insignificant.*

Parlick from Saddle Fell

At the ridge-wall continue down to the waiting saddle, passing rashes of stones on the slopes where Nick's Chair sits flat-topped beyond most of them. At a cluster of stiles and access notice, one could circumvent Parlick's summit by taking the track curving round to the left. More inviting, however, is the prospect of the short pull by the fence to gain the summit at 1417ft/432m. *Though a rather ordinary top, its situation is anything but. The panorama from the pile of stones is outstanding. Anti-clockwise are the West Pennine Moors, South Pennines, Longridge Fell, Pendle Hill, Easington Fell and round via Saddle Fell to the Bleasdale moors. Looking back, Fair Snape's west top is now impressive.*

Leave by the path heading south-east to quickly encounter steep ground, with the waiting Fell Foot Farm directly below. *Parlick (Parlick Pike is its rarely used Sunday name) is a haunt of hang-gliders, and if in evidence they add further colour to the scene. As Parlick is popular with 'normal' visitors too, the path up its steep flank is rather worn.* On encountering the traversing path, take advantage of its easy gradients and turn down right on one of its sunken ways, thence doubling back to the base of the fell. *This not only helps prevent erosion, it makes a more civilised descent.*

At Fell Foot pass through the gate and down the lane. At a junction keeps straight on to a T-junction with Fish House Lane. Cross straight over to a stile and follow a crumbling wall away. This curves down Lingey Hill to be replaced by a few trees and a tiny brook. At a fence, the old way is impassable, and a stile in the fence ahead sees you down the fieldside, crossing a tiny side-stream en route. Approaching a barn (After Lee) cross the beck to a wall-stile, and rise to a part hidden stile by a kink in the fence above. Head directly away from this - with Springs House over to the right - to a stile onto its drive. Turn left to join a back road, and follow this right, soon emerging back into the village.

Brabin's School, Chipping

BLEASDALE FELLS

START *Fell Foot   Grid ref. SD 601442*

DISTANCE *9 miles (14^{1}2km)*

ORDNANCE SURVEY MAPS
1:50,000
Landranger 102 - Preston & Blackpool
1:25,000
Explorer OL41 - Forest of Bowland & Ribblesdale

ACCESS *Start from a popular parking area just before the road end at Fell Foot, almost two miles to the north-west of Chipping.*
• *OPEN ACCESS - see page 9.*

> *An absorbing exploration of lovely Bleasdale, from its farms and fields to its splendid fellside paths*

From the road junction rise a few paces up the cul-de-sac road to a stile on the left. Slant across the field centre, rising gently through reeds to a ladder-stile in the wall ahead. *Already you have extensive views beyond Beacon Fell to Lancashire's plains, with the cone of Parlick just above you.* Head away, joining a fenceside green track on the left. When the fence turns away the track also fades, but keep straight on, over a tiny stream and on above the head of a tiny tree-lined clough to a stile ahead. Now cross a part reedy pasture towards a gate at the end, but slant above it to find a wall-stile. Again keep on to the end, this time bearing right to a stile beyond a stream at the corner. Advance just a little further along the fieldtop to cross a stile alongside an access sign.

Go left along the base of the fell, rapidly leaving the access area at a gate. An inviting green way continues on, rising slightly and looking down on the farm at Blindhurst. A minor brow is reached revealing a stupendous Bleasdale prospect. This features your ascent onto Fair Snape Fell from Higher Fair Snape, the dark Bleasdale moors beyond, and Bleasdale church conspicuous between clumps of trees in the green amphitheatre. Rounding the brow, cross a sunken way ascending from farm to fell, and your own way becomes sunken as it begins to slant right down the flank of the hill. Dropping to a firmer track below, cross the stile behind and drop right to another track. Shortly after fording a small stream bear left off the track, slanting down to a stile. Aiming for the farm at Higher Fair Snape ahead, cross the large field to a stand of trees which shelters a footbridge on the River Brock. Here it is a tiny stream that could be crossed with a single stride.

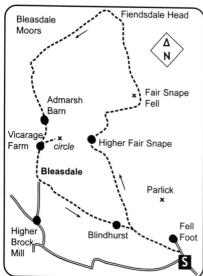

Just behind is a stile back into the fields. Rise away with a fence and watercourse on your left, soon crossing the fence at a stile and resuming on a grassy track up the other side. This runs on the fieldsides to join a surfaced farm road. Turn right to enter Higher Fair Snape. *Features here include mullioned windows on the first house and a coat of arms above the door of the second.* Just above is a fork of paths. Take the right branch, a concession path bound for Fair Snape Fell. It rises a little then turns right through a gate to run beneath modern barns. At the end a fenced track rises away to emerge into a field. It then ascends the fieldside, through a gate and up to a gate at the top. Winding grandly up another field to a gate onto rougher fell slopes, the track slants right for a delightful rise to a stile onto the true fell.

Continuing briefly with the wall, it quickly doubles back to commence a classic zigzag on a brilliantly made way up the fell. Effortlessly reaching the top, it peters out on the moor edge just as a faint pathway is joined. This runs left 150 yards to the waiting west top of Fair Snape Fell. At 1673ft/510m this is not the true summit of Fair Snape, which stands less enticingly at the watershed fence junction to the north-east. *This is, however, most certainly the place to be, as two cairns and an Ordnance Survey column play second fiddle to a practical stone shelter. Paddy's Pole, as marked on maps, is - intermittently, it seems - embedded in the sprawling cairn. The view has now opened out to embrace a distant Lakeland skyline beyond the nearer hills of Three Peaks Country.*

As the section from Fair Snape to Fiendsdale Head features in WALK 7, consider this pathless alternative which proves thoroughly enjoyable and far less messy. The idea is to slant round the fellside to meet the path from Fiendsdale Head. You should be pathless all the way, but also peat-free! Simply set off in a direction slightly west of north, soon encountering a fence ideally where it is crossed by a stile. Resume slanting round, only gently losing height as you cross tiny watercourses, all the while enjoying springy turf and short-cropped heather. Your objective is the principal stream at the head of the Brock's western arm, a delightful little Pennine clough.

You should be sufficiently near the top to cross effortlessly, thence rising gently away to quickly encounter the Fiendsdale-Bleasdale path, conveniently after it has escaped the peaty felltop. Turning left down this, it quickly dries into a stony path slanting down the fell. *Fair Snape Fell increases in grandeur with every step.* Suddenly the path transforms into a smooth green rake as it slants through lush bilberry bushes. *Over to the left, Parlick reveals itself from behind Fair Snape.* Meeting the intake wall at the bottom, go forward with it until reaching a stile in it.

Turn down the field to meet a drive between Holme House and Hazelhurst. Though the next stile is in the centre of the fence directly below, the right of way officially goes right a short way along the drive before turning down to it. Descend the large field to another stile in the bottom corner, behind which adjacent foot-bridges are crossed before a track runs to Admarsh Barn Farm. Pass left of the buildings to emerge onto the drive, which leads out to Vicarage Farm. Over to the left, sequestered in trees, is Bleasdale stone circle. Situated on private land, it is reached by a concession path leaving the road at a kissing-gate opposite the farm. Pass round the left side of the field to a kissing-gate at the far end, then cross to the clump of trees enclosing the circle: another kissing-gate gives access to the hidden confines, and an information panel.

Perhaps 3000 years old, the circle was discovered a century ago by a local farmer. A 150ft diameter ditch encircles the burial mound, in which two cremations were found in urns. Low concrete pillars have replaced the original 11 oak posts that surrounded it. Back at Vicarage Farm, head out along the drive to quickly reach the church. *St Eadmer's dates from 1835, and was restored later that century. The first chapel stood here in 1637. The dedication is unique: Eadmor was biographer of several saints, including Anselm and Wilfred. He died in 1124, still a simple monk.*

Back on the road go a little further to the village hall and school, then after the sports field a stile sends a path left through reedy ground to a sliver of woodland. Emerging into a vast field, bear right to a gate at the corner onto the Fairsnape farms road. Go briefly left, and at the cattle-grid turn right along a fenceside. This curves round to the corner where a footbridge on the Brock, seat and wall-stile await. Across, head away with the gurgling stream, then continue to a gate ahead. A firm track runs towards Blindhurst, climbing a final enclosure to the farm. Entering the cobbled yard, bear left after the principal house. *The attractive white frontage sports mullioned and transomed windows and a 1731 datestone.* From a gate back out, at once leave the track and rise right to a gate. Continue rising, briefly, then commence a long, steady slant across this large, sloping field, crossing a small stream midway and on to a stile in the far corner. Now back upon the outward route, turn right to retrace steps through the fields.

St Eadmer's,
Bleasdale

RIVER BROCK

START *Beacon Fell*   *Grid ref. SD 564426*

DISTANCE *6¹4 miles (10km)*

ORDNANCE SURVEY MAPS
1:50,000
Landranger 102 - Preston & Blackpool
1:25,000
Explorer OL41 - Forest of Bowland & Ribblesdale

ACCESS *Start from the Bowland Visitor Centre at Beacon Fell Country Park (west of Chipping). Large car park.*

> *The wooded banks of the River Brock offer a rare opportunity for an extended riverside ramble. Go at bluebell time!*

Beacon Fell opened in 1970 as Lancashire's first country park, a valued and well-used amenity comprising 185 acres of moorland and woodland. The visitor centre provides information, displays, shop, refreshments and WC. Outside is a sculpture by Thompson Dagnall entitled 'Ormé Sight', unveiled in 1995 to commemorate its first 25 years. Though various short walks offer scope for exploring the fell, it is too small to plan a decent walk within its confines. Leave by crossing the road to the lower car park, then take a stile on its right side, on the edge of trees, to emerge into a large sloping field. *Savour sweeping views of the Ribble estuary and surrounding plains.* Descend the fieldside to a ladder-stile, and continue to a stile in the bottom corner. This sends a path through trees, running neatly down a streamside (bedecked with bluebells) to the white-walled house at Salisbury, and out along its drive.

Turn left along Bleasdale Road, and keep right to pass Eccles Moss Farm, with its striking frontage. At the next junction keep straight on Stannalee Lane, passing further residential interest at

Higher Stannalee Cottage with its thatched roof. Keep on past more isolated dwellings to a sharp bend left at another house, Rake Head, then turn sharp right on a path shrouded in greenery. It descends an old hollowed way to the environs of the river at Brock Bottom, amid much bluebell cover in season. Cross a footbridge to the low ruins of millworkers' cottages and one of four nearby mills the Brock served. *All succumbed to steam powered mills on the plain below.* Head upstream on the Brock Valley Nature Trail. Very popular at weekends, this super walk runs up to the Brock car park and picnic area at Higher Brock Bridge. *This is a minor culture shock, being gained suddenly after the woodland surrounds.*

Cross over the bridge and turn upstream, below a house dubbed Brock Mill. A stile after Brock Mill Cottage puts you into a field which is crossed to cut a bend of the river before rejoining it at a stile in the far corner. Enclosed by a fence, the path now clings tightly to its bank through a lovely stretch, until a marshy area is approached where it turns to climb the bank. Rising to

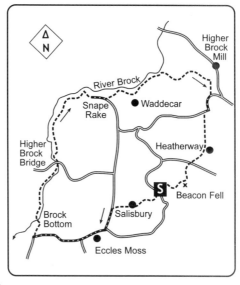

meet a firm track, follow this left. This overlooks an aqueduct that carries Manchester's pipeline from Thirlmere, then the track drops to an isolated building. Passing to its right, a path runs along the foot of a wooded bank. At the end the wooded riverbank resumes for a grand stroll to a footbridge at Snape Rake. *The ford here was used by the Romans on their route from Ribchester to Lancaster.*

Without crossing, turn right up the hollowed way, climbing steeply to a dead-end road which is followed away. Beacon Fell becomes prominent directly ahead. At the end of the wood on the left, re-enter at the last moment on a part sunken bridleway that slants back down. As it doubles sharply back left, walkers take a choice of ways. The public footpath keeps straight on, scrambling over a tiny stream to a field corner, then along to the end to pick up a track descending from Waddecar. More popular is the bridleway continuing down to the valley floor, advancing to the riverbank to turn upstream: the bridleway crosses the river at some unclear point, leaving an unofficial path to continue upstream to a big clearing to pick up the scout track. *Various features hereabouts show evidence of this being part of the county scout campsite.*

Continuing upstream, a footpath leaves the track to cling to the riverbank, and the track peters out approaching a stile out of the trees. A faint path continues through a couple of fields to a footbridge. *This last stage offers open views, with Fair Snape Fell filling the frame ahead. The bridge spans the southernmost of the two infant Brock streams at their confluence.* Don't cross, but turn right past a substantial low ruin to a stile, and a path continues upstream through a landslip in the trees. Quickly you find yourself on a feeder of the main stream, and the path runs to a bridge. Across, it slants up the wooded clough to a stile at the top, out into the open. Head directly away, bearing slightly left with a broken line of hawthorns, aiming for the cone of Parlick directly in front.

Eccles
Moss
Farm

Now you have splendid open views, with little Beacon Fell upstaged by the outstanding picture of the Bleasdale cirque. The old hedge turns away just yards short of a gate ahead. Now simply follow the fence on your left rising faintly on. Reaching a muddy junction at the end, pass through a couple of stiles and turn right along the fenceside to the house at Wickens Barn (1850 datestone). The path diverts to its left to emerge onto Oakenclough Road. Turn right, and leave at the first opportunity by a farm drive rising away. Follow this to the big house at the top, Heatherway. Now take a stile on the right, and within a minute, at a break in the fence, a waymark sends a thin path up the large pasture to a stile at the top. It continues up open ground to the road encircling Beacon Fell.

Virtually opposite, a forest road slants right up through the plantation. Emerging into daylight at a junction with a biking trail, turn left a short way then take a path rising right through a few trees to a bridle-gate onto open moorland. It climbs to a second gate, immediately above which stands the Ordnance Survey column crowning Beacon Fell at the modest height of 872ft/266m. *Affixed to its top is a view indicator: some of its features are distinctly under-represented thanks to the growth of trees to south and east, though everything one wants to see is readily on display. The fell is named from its former role, as a beacon site for perhaps 1000 years: it was part of the chain that warned of the approach of the Spanish Armada in 1588.* To finish, follow the main path into the trees, over a cross-paths and down, it swings right at the bottom to re-enter the open ground surrounding the visitor centre.

Beacon Fell, looking to Fair Snape Fell and Parlick

13

NICKY NOOK

START Scorton   Grid ref. SD 504503

DISTANCE 5^3_4 miles (9km)

ORDNANCE SURVEY MAPS
1:50,000
Landranger 102 - Preston & Blackpool
1:25,000
Explorer OL41 - Forest of Bowland & Ribblesdale

ACCESS Start from Scorton picnic site/car park on Clevely Bank Lane, one mile north of the village alongside the motorway. Scorton is served by bus from Garstang.

> *Exploring a miniature fell on Bowland's western fringe, with glorious moorland views and a fine little valley*

Return to the road and turn left over the motorway. *At once pause to appraise the fell country ahead. To the right is Nicky Nook, and ahead Harrisend Fell rising to the higher moors. Far over to the left are the Abbeystead Moors crowned by Ward's Stone, with Clougha Pike and Grit Fell supporting it.* Keep left at the junction ahead, passing the delightful thatched Bland's Cottage. Within five minutes, at a sharp bend, turn sharp right along an unsigned back road. This leafy way runs on for some way before turning sharply up to the left. Here keep straight on a stony drive, passing Wyresdale Lake which presents an attractive foreground to Nicky Nook. These grounds are part of Wyresdale Hall, and soon Home Farm is passed before emerging onto Snowhill Lane amid dense woodland at the entrance drive to the big house of Wyresdale Park. Turn sharply left on it, crossing a stream and climbing steeply to a T-junction.

Cross the stile ahead from where a path climbs directly up the fell through rampant gorse bushes. *This is colourful country: looking back over the plain, observe the Wyreside Lakes, Heysham power station, Lancaster University, the M6 motorway, Blackpool Tower, a wide sweep of Morecambe Bay, and a massive line of the distant Lakeland Fells. To the left, meanwhile, is the great Ward's Stone skyline.* Through a kissing-gate alongside an attractive small reservoir, open country is entered. Advance to the brow, and with a small stand of Scots Pine ahead the path bears right, bound for the waiting Ordnance Survey column on Nicky Nook. *The reedy pool of The Tarn below makes a fine foreground to Ward's Stone.*

Over a crossroads of ways the path surmounts a broad ridge, passing a large cairn before reaching the trig point. At a modest 705ft/215m this is the summit of the walk. *Ahead now is a fine moorland prospect, with the upper reaches of the River Calder burrowing deep into Hawthornthwaite Fell and the Bleasedale Moors. A contrasting feature of the 360-degree panorama is* the flatness of The Fylde, including Garstang and the motorway: indeed it seems Grize Dale is the only thing you can't see.

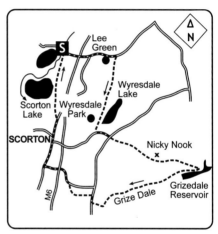

The path continues away towards a wall. Ignore the stile and bear right to the wall corner, at once reaching the edge of a steep drop. *Stone towers in the vicinity mark the line of the Thirlmere Aqueduct on its journey from Lakeland to Manchester.* A glorious moment, with Grizedale Reservoir shimmering in the wooded bowl of Grize Dale. *Nicky Nook's finest hour is especially resplendent in spring or autumn colour.* Slowly descend the clear path to a stile onto a solid track. Turn right here to commence a splendid tramp along the dale, initially alongside the small reservoir. *Grize Dale comes from 'gris' dale meaning valley of the wild pigs. Grizedale Brook is born in the cradle of Bowland's westernmost moors, and runs a good five miles to join the River Wyre just short of Garstang.* The broad path declines very gently as it runs a glorious course along the valley floor, partly through woodland, and with the stream for company. Enjoy some splendid open views of the fellside, which appears far greater than its modest scale actually is. Ultimately the path runs to a footbridge under a small scar. Don't cross, but from the stile turn sharp right across the field. The path slants up beneath a wooded bank to a kissing-gate onto a back road, Higher Lane.

Go right, briefly, and just past the houses at Slean End take a stile in the hedge on the left. Descend the field, bearing right to a corner stile above Wyresdale Cottage. Now slant across towards its drive, a pair of stiles giving access to it as it joins Tithe Barn Lane. Turn down through an attractive cluster of dwellings (Tithebarn Cottage is the old tithe barn) to drop beneath the motorway to a junction with Gubberford Lane. Cross to the footway and turn right into the village, passing the tall-spired church as you go.

How times have changed at Scorton, which long since lost its station on the Preston to Lancaster rail line, but to no benefit of its own gained the near parallel M6 motorway. This nevertheless remains a pleasant little spot focused around a large hotel, the Priory, with its public bar the Stouts Inn. It has a Post office/shop, a giftshop/coffee shop and WC. Keep straight on and out the other end, a verge assisting when the footway terminates. Just past the de-restriction signs a path is signed left, crossing a footbridge and swinging sharp right to shadow the stream.

Two further bridges in quick succession are encountered before advancing to a gate/stile ahead. Bear across the left side of the broadening field, with Scorton Lake to your left. Its outflow into a big marsh on the right is crossed and on over a stile to the far corner where a stile awaits. The now firm path runs along a wood edge, emerging at the end onto an access road. Bear right on this through woodland to rejoin the narrow road alongside Cleveley Bridge on the River Wyre. The start is just a minute along to the right, with the possibility of refreshments at the fishery along to the left.

GRIZEDALE HEAD

START *Grizedale Bridge*   *Grid ref. SD 536490*

DISTANCE *6¹2 miles (10¹2km)*

ORDNANCE SURVEY MAPS
1:50,000
Landranger 102 - Preston & Blackpool
1:25,000
Explorer OL41 - Forest of Bowland & Ribblesdale

ACCESS *Start from the car park on the north side of the bridge, on the Dolphinholme-Oakenclough road.* • *OPEN ACCESS - see page 9.*

Moorland walking on Bowland's western fringe with a contrast of good paths and no paths. Great views over the Fylde

The small, stone arched Grizedale Bridge spans Grizedale Brook where it leaves the rolling moors for the better frequented surrounds of Nicky Nook (see WALK 13). Information panels and seats contribute to this popular motorists' halt. Begin by heading north up the gently rising moor-edge road across the foot of Harrisend Fell. *At once you can view a massive seascape, with Morecambe Bay fronting the Lakeland hills from Black Combe round to the Coniston Fells*. After breaking fully free, abandon the road by descending a green track to the left. At the bottom it fades, but turning right it reasserts itself to continue clearly on a contour along the moor, passing above a young plantation. As this ends cross to a plantation corner just ahead, here picking up a footpath rising from the farm at Fell End. This takes you gently half-right back up onto the moorland road. *By now you have a panorama stretching from Blackpool Tower to Lakeland's Eastern Fells*.

Cross to a well-defined little path running a mercurial course across the fell, largely through luxuriant bilberry, maintaining its contour as the road drops away. *Curving gently around a brow, the views increase over Ward's Stone and upper Wyre country.* Reaching a fence corner, advance to the recessed corner just ahead where a kissing-gate leads off the moor. Here begins a long half-mile, largely level crossing of the fields. Cross the field bottom, towards the end taking a gate on the left. Follow a track briefly before abandoning its descent in favour of a stile on the right. Cross towards the wooded clough ahead, dropping into it (ignore a stile ahead into trees) to cross the stream and slant up the bank to a little corner gate. Resume on the field bottom, and from a stile at the end a footbridge crosses a little tree-lined clough. Crossing a narrow pasture to the next stile, advance along one final field bottom to a wall-stile onto a bend of the Scorton-Marshaw road.

Bear right on the road, emerging onto Catshaw Fell at a cattle-grid. Keep straight on the grassy verge, passing an attractive reedy pool and steadily dropping down. *Ahead are views over the Wyre's beginnings to the Ward's Stone skyline.* At a corner, slip down to join a track to the right as it bridges the stream. Through a gate behind, the track runs a delec-

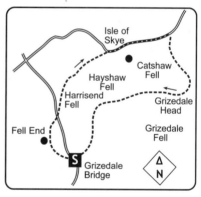

table grassy course across the moor to Catshaw Greave. Here the way receives a harder surface to begin a steep climb above the main left-hand branch. *Landmarks as diverse as Heysham power station and the Langdale Pikes feature in your retrospective panorama.* Very early, however, opt to leave the hard track in favour of the heather tongue of Pig's Face to your right. A distinct zigzagging old track can be seen scaling it, so choose a spot to drop to the stream - ideally just above a lone rowan - and scale the bank behind to gain the old way. Its only users today are sheep, though its sunken course, filled with easy-going bilberry bushes, is clear as you zigzag up onto flatter ground.

Following the bank above the right-hand clough (Far Greave Clough), the way fades on these gentler contours. *By now you can appraise further diverse features such as the Lune Estuary and the massive Abbeystead mansion in trees in front of Ward's Stone.* As this clough too has now split (Near Greave Clough swings more up to the left), drop down again to cross the tiny clough onto a level tongue (the further clough has stone butts alongside). Rise away, yet again with a clough on your right, though there is little point in crossing this third one, as almost at once it fades onto a virtually flat moortop. Up ahead can be seen the watershed fence on Grizedale Head, while just to your right is the terminus of another shooters' road. Simply cross to the fence, joining at a kissing-gate.

Don't pass through, simply turn right alongside the fence for a stretch of heather bashing. Cross the flat top of Grizedale Head (the high point of the walk at 1207ft/368m) and the ground gently declines, sometimes aided by faint trods and grassier stretches. *With the scent of heather in your nostrils savour massive views of peaks and plains, moors and bays.* Remain with this fence all the way, passing a boundary stone inscribed 'Hayshaw TLF 1846' at a fence junction. *Observant eyes will note the map's identification of 'stones with inscriptions' down to the right. Having sought them out, I can advise there are at least a further four, all identical to this one: their purpose seems to be to mark the boundary between Hayshaw and Catshaw Fells.* A short rise leads to a cairn at around 1100ft/335m on Hayshaw Fell, before advancing to a kissing-gate on the end. This offers a wider panorama still.

Here is a minor dilemma as you remain with the fence dropping left. Passing through the gate allows access to another gate lower down, thus avoiding a fence junction below where you must step over: the anomaly is that the going is easier on the right side - the choice is yours! As you descend, the wild upper reaches of Grizedale drive deep into the Abbeystead moors. Lower down, below the fence junction and the gate, a path forms after crossing a little clough, though it fades before reaching Grizedale Intake at the bottom. Simply turn right, downstream with Grizedale Brook, for the final section along the base of the fell, encountering an occasional trod as you wander back to the start.

WARD'S STONE

START *Abbeystead*   *Grid ref. SD 563543*

DISTANCE *9 miles (14¹⁄₂km)*

ORDNANCE SURVEY MAPS
1:50,000
Landranger 102 - Preston & Blackpool
1:25,000
Explorer OL41 - Forest of Bowland & Ribblesdale

ACCESS *Start from a small parking area at Stoops Bridge, at the eastern end of the hamlet. Served by bus from Lancaster. • OPEN ACCESS - see page 9.*

> *A classic moorland trek to the summit of Bowland.*
> *The ascent and return are on firm tracks, leaving only*
> *a modest amount of 'wilder' moorland rambling*

Abbeystead takes its name from an involvement with Furness Abbey. Today it is an architecturally interesting and very private hamlet. A school was founded in 1674: look also for the pinfold. Nearby Abbeystead Lake was constructed in 1853 to supply water for mills on the Wyre plains. The Duke of Westminster's estate office administers some 20,000 acres of grouse moorland. From the charming setting of the two-arched bridge on the Tarnbrook Wyre, head along the side road very briefly, then turn left on a track along the edge of trees. This quickly runs to a gate into a field, which is crossed almost to the far end. As you bear right to a footbridge, ahead is the enormous house of Abbeystead. *Built in 1886 for the Earl of Sefton, its bold Elizabethan-style south front overlooks extensive grounds and is well seen from the path. Just below here the two founders of the Wyre finally merge to form the main river just prior to its entry into Abbeystead Lake.*

Cross the bridge over the Marshaw Wyre and bear left, rising gently across a large pasture well above the stream, looking across to the Abbeystead grounds. As they end, drop left to a footbridge back over the Marshaw Wyre. Ascend a steep bank of gorse and scrub to cross to ladder-stiles either side of a driveway. In the next field bear gently right to a path crossroads at a fence corner, to find a stile in the little recess to the right. Follow the fence away on a distinct bank, and through a gate at the end advance to a stile in a hedge in front, just to the right of the farm at Higher Emmetts.

Cross the road and on the short drive to Top of Emmetts. Don't enter, but take a stile on the right and head away with the hedge. From a stile in the very corner briefly follow a fence, then cross a hedge by stiles into a large, reedy pasture. *The moorland miles of Ward's Stone are outspread ahead.* Slant diagonally down to a stile in the corner. Pass right of a barn and down the hedgeside, along several fields to a short access lane behind Ouzel Thorn Farm. Cross to a stile opposite and

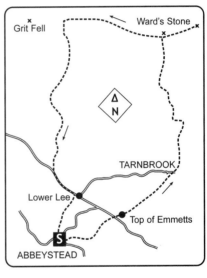

over a small field to a wall-stile, overlooking an attractive bend of the Tarnbrook Wyre. Advance along the small enclosure to a gate at the end, then left on a concrete farm bridge and out along a short walled lane to meet the road in the hamlet of Tarnbrook. *This peaceful old Quaker settlement was much busier when felt hats and gloves were manufactured here.*

Cross straight over and alongside the green to a gate at a range of access signs. Head away on the splendid track, which charts an unfailing course up through several pastures, each featuring very different vegetation as you approach moorland terrain. The top gate sees you onto the moor proper. Simply remain on the track as it winds up bouldery, bilberry slopes, past a shooters' cabin and up to a junction with a hard road. *Constructed in Spring 2005, this completes a network of unsightly roads.* Ignore the right branch and rise to a second junction just above. *If you want to opt out, go left here for an easy stroll that slowly descends to meet the return route.* Ignoring the left branch, continue uphill on the steep track which abruptly terminates above Tarnsyke Clough. A thin trod rises away from it through the heather, but quickly swings right to cross the stream, which is not much help. Instead continue directly up, this being the only heather-bashing section of the entire walk.

Here you might encounter the black-headed gulls that nest nearby, adding variety to the call of grouse and other moorland birds. The grouse must have called less happily here on the 'Glorious' Twelfth of 1915, when, with tens of thousands of young men dying in distant trenches, a record bag of almost 3000 birds was claimed. The fell was subjected to further barrages when used for army training during the second almighty conflict. Uncontrollable fires in August 1947 supposedly put paid to any unexploded shells remaining!

The Ward's Stone plateau forms the skyline ahead, only a short distance across increasingly easy terrain marked by random cairns. On gentle slopes bear steadily left past stony outcrops of differing sizes as grass replaces heather, ultimately rising on cushioned turf to suddenly find the West top just ahead, marked by an Ordnance Survey column at 1837ft/560m. Just past it is Ward's Stone itself, a grand outcrop on which to scramble, and a useful shelter.

The 360-degree panorama is one to take in slowly: Three Peaks Country, the Lakeland Fells, Morecambe Bay, and of course the complete mass of Bowland itself. Having surveyed this, thoughts can turn to the girth of the plateau. Hopefully you will relish the 'out-and-back' mile's walk to the East top, partly because it's the summit but also because it offers the day's finest walking! On setting off the path briefly becomes faint, but remains a delectable grassy way: the easiest walking of this moorland route leads directly across to the far side, past one or two peat castles, pools, and an occasional cairn. *This crossing engenders a feeling of being not merely on a moortop, but also a real fell.*

The second OS column is quickly reached on the corresponding eastern edge of the plateau. *Looking back, that first column now appears higher, surely? In fact, the OS map claims this point is 1840ft/561m, one metre higher than the first - though Ward's Stone itself might have something to say on the issue. Either way, you have traversed the crest of Bowland. The main change in the view is the replacement of the coastal scene with a better picture of Three Peaks Country. In the immediate environs are the Grey Mare and Foal outcrops surmounted by a cairn and stake.*

To resume, return to the West top, just beyond which the path transforms into a surprisingly eroded way dropping through a stone-capped scarp and then more steadily across the broad watershed on Cabin Flat. Ahead is Grit Fell's dome, but well before that your level path passes a pool and falters just short of a firm shooters' track. Turn left here to commence what will prove a rapid return. The track soon starts to slant downhill, with Ward's Stone looming large to your left. It drops steeply above a small clough and a shooters' box to a junction with the track met on the ascent.

Continue straight down, passing a waterworks stone of 1852 just to the left. The moorland proper is soon left behind at a gate in a wall on a brow. Like the ascent route, the way is infallible as the improving track runs down varied pastures. Past a plantation it swings sharply right to the elegant house at Higher Lee. Its short drive leads quickly out onto a road, where go left down to Lower Lee. *Just to the left is Lower Lee House, dating from 1694 and at one time an inn.* Don't cross the

bridge but take a gate on the right, from where a broad track makes a pleasant conclusion as it runs through two pastures, the second having the environs of the Tarnbrook Wyre for company, and with a bluebell wood on the right. The track leads you to a wall-stile onto the road just yards from the bridge where the walk began.

The Tarnbrook Wyre

CLOUGHA PIKE

START *Quernmore*   *Grid ref. SD 526604*

DISTANCE *6³4 miles (11km)*

ORDNANCE SURVEY MAPS
1:50,000
Landranger 97 - Kendal to Morecambe
Landranger 102 - Preston & Blackpool
1:25,000
Explorer OL41 - Forest of Bowland & Ribblesdale

ACCESS *Start from Birk Bank car park on Rigg Lane, a mile north-east of Quernmore crossroads. Quernmore is served by bus from Lancaster. • OPEN ACCESS - see page 9.*

A colourful walk on Bowland's north-western moors, visiting a splendid viewpoint atop uncharacteristically rugged terrain

The name Quernmore comes from querns, or millstones, hewn from the local rock for grinding corn. In other instances the name has evolved into 'Whern', as in Whernside in the Yorkshire Dales. Nearby Brow Top offers various attractions, including a craft centre, tearoom, and some interesting animals. It was around here that Roman kilns - or hypocausts - have been discovered, complete with bricks, tiles and pots still in the ovens.

From a gate at the back of the car park follow the track rising away. Ahead is the rocky Birk Bank, still regenerating after the activities of the quarries. *250 years ago, Clougha slates were in great demand for roofing.* At a fork bear right (merely a brief short-cut back onto the grassy track) and then right again on the track running to a gate. Don't go through but take the path down to the left, using boards to cross a marsh to a stile. A well-used path starts to climb the fell, initially through gorse and oak and alongside a stream. Rising past the great bank of the old quarry, the path becomes more solid to climb through rampant bilberries to a wall junction beneath a rocky knoll. Here is a choice of stiles. *That to the right sends a more direct and easier route towards the top.* That to the left holds more interest, and is described here.

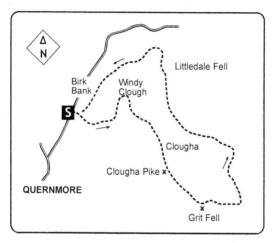

Over the stile you enter Windy Clough's atmospheric confines. Whilst you can meander along the bottom, better to take a thin branch path left within fifty yards of the stile. This winds faintly up to meet the wall on the rocky crest. *By now the summit of Clougha Pike is on show to the south-east, the OS column possibly bright in the sun. The trench of Windy Clough was formed by glacial melt-water towards the end of the Ice Age.* A thin trod traverses this smashing little ridge atop a gritstone edge, looking dramatically over the clough to the slopes of Clougha. *Caton Moor windfarm is visible to the north, with the contrasting (in every sense) frame of Heysham power station seen to the west.* A tiny patch of oakwood at the end leads to a wall corner. Turn down the wallside to find a kissing-gate in it at the head of the clough. Across it a thin path simply follows the wall up to the right: initially extremely steep and intermittently rocky, it is virtually a mini-scramble.

Things ease up in the heather above as the trod clings to the wall. A smaller amphitheatre precedes two pronounced notches, both offering rougher going if taken direct: the main path performs a loop round to the left, rejoining the wall at a ladder-stile ahead. Across it comes a fine moment, with Clougha's upper contours fully revealed in front, promising a splendid ramble above a slanting bouldery edge to its waiting top. The path cuts a corner of the wall, shortly after which it is reinforced by the easier path from below, to rise only ever steadily. *Throughout this ascent the views are magnificent, looking over the Vale of Quernmore to the silvery waters of Morecambe Bay backed by a skyline of Lakeland Fells.*

The wall falters at the onset of a rocky edge, and a fence branches off left. The main path simply continues to a prominent cairn, from where the summit waits just beyond. *At 1355ft/413m this is a busy place, an OS column sharing the platform with some sprawling shelters taking advantage of the rash of stones. The fact that level ground heads away to the heathery hinterland is no real concern on your 'pikeless' pike. As a viewpoint it adds little to the magnificent scene that has already been enjoyed, save for the inclusion of more moorland, inland to Ward's Stone's great top beyond nearer Grit Fell. The value of a view indicator adorning the trig point is questionable: whilst including the entirely irrelevant 'Settle 21m' (hidden far beyond a whole range of Bowland's moors), there is no mention of the finest landmark, Ingleborough, there for all to see!*

Leave by the clearest path heading away, running east to the fence, bound for Grit Fell. Over a stile in it the path swings right and on through the heather. At the low point here, a cairn marks the departure of a thin trod down to the left, offering a useful short-cut that points you to the shooters' road visible just minutes below. Otherwise, make the short rise to a fence corner above. Over a stile the path rises the short way to another fence corner. *A minute's detour further right along the fence permits a visit to the massive cairn of Shooters Pile perched on a rash of stones.* Cross the stile alongside a boundary stone and trace the path away through the heather: you are virtually atop Grit Fell from the out-set, though the cairn stands a little down the slope beyond. *At 1535ft/468m this is emphatically the high point of the day, though it's really only an add-on: Clougha Pike remains the star.*

Past the cairn the path descends to the wastes of Cabin Flat, with a big Ward's Stone skyline ahead. You go only as far as a hard shooters' road in the dip. Turning left, this remains underfoot for almost three miles. Keep left when an early fork goes right, and the track curves around the moor and then down to a second fork. Keep left again, briefly rising to the environs of an old quarry site. *Just above is the once busy central area: an intriguing arrangement of modern stone edifices was the work of sculptor Andy Goldsworthy around the turn of the Millennium.* Through further extensive spoil heaps the track leaves to swing downhill, enjoying vast views and passing close by several tall beacons on the left.

Ultimately the road winds sharply down into a dry hollow, passing through a gate to run more pleasantly on down to a gate in a wall at the boundary of access land. Do not pass through however, but turn left on a broad, grassy track which runs along the bottom of the moorland, above a birch wooded corner and along to Ottergear Bridge, a stone aqueduct high above the stream. Cross it to re-enter the Birk Bank moorland, and a level path heads away. Virtually level throughout, this forms a delightful conclusion as it traverses richly colourful terrain (a robust mix of heather, grass, bilberry, gorse, birch, rocks, scrub) to lead back beneath the bank to rejoin the outward route just a couple of minutes from the start.

Clougha Pike from the approach path

LITTLEDALE

START Little Cragg   Grid ref. SD 546617

DISTANCE 6^{1}4 miles (10km)

ORDNANCE SURVEY MAPS
1:50,000
Landranger 97 - Kendal to Morecambe
1:25,000
Explorer OL41 - Forest of Bowland & Ribblesdale

ACCESS Start from Little Cragg car park, on a minor road linking Brookhouse and Quernmore. Approach from Brookhouse (off the A683 at Caton) by Littledale Road (2^{1}2 miles from the village).
• OPEN ACCESS - see page 9.

> *Along with a delectable moorland spell this walk features much fine woodland, and more to the point, an unforgettable array of bluebells. Call it the Bluebell Walk!*

Having already enjoyed grand views while pulling your boots on, head east from the car park back towards Brookhouse. Through a cattle-grid with Cragg Farm on the right, the narrow road winds down through rough pasture. *Savour fine views over Morecambe Bay to an unbroken skyline, from Black Combe through the Lakeland Fells and right round to Great Coum in Yorkshire's Three Peaks Country: Caton Moor windfarm is also on show across Littledale.* This minor road becomes enclosed again to descend to the charming wooded surrounds of a confluence of becks, with the first of the bluebells in evidence.

Udale and Fostal Bridges are crossed in succession, passing Littledale scout camp before a short pull up (vast bluebell carpets on the left) and along to a crossroads at New House Farm. Turn right, passing through the hamlet of Crossgill. *The farmhouse bears a 1661 datestone: another pleasing house stands before the drive to Littledale Hall. Just past it is Littledale's tiny former church. Dating from 1751, St Ann's is now a private dwelling.*

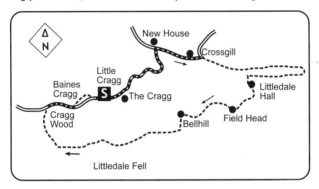

Beyond the old church is a hairpin bend: turn off through a stile to follow a splendid green pathway between plantations. At the end keep straight on to approach a church sat in the middle of a field. This Free Church of 1849 was attached to nearby Littledale Hall. *Now merely a shell, its intact stonework and timber ceiling are appreciated by the sheep that find sanctuary within. The evidence of the last ten minutes suggests that The Almighty has fallen from favour in Littledale! At the back is a solitary grave. The intact one of two slabs marks the resting place of father and son Dodsons of the hall, the unfortunate son having beaten his father here by 39 years.* Just beyond, the track forks: the main one drops down to Littledale Hall, to which you shall shortly return.

For now however, take the inviting grassy branch up to the left. Remain along the fieldtop when the track goes through a gate, and keep on to a little gate to run inside the top of a wooded bank. A delectable little path ambles above an exquisite bluebell carpet. Emerging at a stile, a grand scene greets the eye with Ragill Beck splashing along beneath woodland: your return route is seen below, but for now contour on, crossing a tiny stream as you traverse the bracken bank. At the end the path winds down to a sidestream, a nice location for the turning point. Strictly speaking, the path fords the stream to a gateway and then turns on the bank behind to drop back down to a stile in the wall. Cross the footbridge and head downstream with Ragill Beck, re-entering the woodland at another stile. *The bluebell display now truly excels.* A stile at the other end precedes arrival back at the arched bridge at Littledale Hall.

Cross to the coach house and turn away from the hall, up through the farmyard. At the last barn at the top, leave by a gate on the right. A grassy track runs upstream with Foxdale Beck - more bluebells! Quickly crossing by a footbridge, a path doubles back to wind up the bank. Leaving the trees at a stile, turn right along the gently rising fenceside. A wall takes over to head towards Field Head Farm. Well before it take a stile in the wall and pass right of the buildings to gain the drive. Following this away it runs over a brow (with magnificent Lakeland views) and down to Bellhill Farm.

Cross the cattle-grid and turn into the yard of the lower house, a barn conversion. At the end pass beneath a small barn and through a small enclosure before heading down the left side of the field on a rough track. Turning right at the bottom it fords a side beck and the more substantial Udale Beck, the latter also having a footbridge. Rise away up the reedy pasture side on the stony track as far as a stile in the fence part way up, from where a green track rises above a belt of trees. It quickly fades but simply keep left along the fieldtop. At the end a stone bridge carries a track over tree-lined Sweet Beck, and just beyond is a junction. Take the inviting branch left, a link path to the open country of Littledale Fell. *For a direct return, remain on the track to Skelbow barn, and along fieldsides to be back at the start within ten minutes.*

*The old church,
Littledale Hall*

The main route turns up the track which rises pleasantly to a stile and along to a ladder-stile onto the foot of the moor. Turn right, crossing a marshy trickle followed by the burbling infant River Conder to a very prominent green way slanting away. *The views rapidly open out into a cacophony of colour. Morecambe Bay and the Lakeland Fells are backdrop to a beautiful foreground of Cragg Wood and the Conder Valley, over which both Baines Cragg and, hopefully, the car should be seen.* As the way falters on the moor edge, simply bear right over adjacent tiny trickles above the heathery edge, and a clear path drops gently to a point where a broader path rises to the edge. This now runs across the moor, becoming a thinner trod running to a point above a prominent group of rocks. This attractive little ravine is a grand spot on a sunny, late summer day, and the trod runs on past it to join a hard shooters' track just beyond.

Turn right as it winds steeply down to a gate/stile in a narrow defile, and down more pleasantly to pass through another gate. Approaching the house ahead, don't take its drive out but go right over a slab bridge to a stile, from where a little path winds up the scrubby bank to a stile onto a road. Turn right alongside lovely Cragg Wood (displaying the walk's final bluebells), initially steeply to reach the open country of Baines Cragg. *With its enthusiastic mix of bracken, heather, bilberry, scrub, rocks, brambles and birch, this slipped the net as Open Country in 2004.* As an inviting alternative to the road, with the start of the rocks just above, you may be tempted to cross to scramble along the crest. *In autumn this must be seen to be believed: colourful foreground leads the eye to Cragg Wood under moorland slopes.* This conclusion winds back to the road, with the car park just over the cattle-grid.

Baines Cragg, looking to Little Cragg

ROEBURNDALE

START Wray   Grid ref. SD 604679

DISTANCE 9 miles (14^{1}2km)

ORDNANCE SURVEY MAPS
1:50,000
Landranger 97 - Kendal to Morecambe
1:25,000
Explorer OL41 - Forest of Bowland & Ribblesdale

ACCESS Start from a riverside parking area at the east entrance to the village, just off the B6480 by the modern bridge. One could also start from the main street. Served by Settle-Lancaster bus.

> An intimate exploration of the valley of the River Roeburn

Wray and the Roeburn are indelibly linked, the river having supplied water power for an industrious past: like the adjacent Hindburn, it is named from the deer that roamed the Forest of Bowland. Attractive cottages line the streets, including many old yeoman houses: a particularly old one inscribed 'RP 1656' refers to Richard Pooley who founded the school. There is also a Friends' Meeting House of 1704. There is a tearoom at Bridge House Farm on the edge of the village, and a second pub, the Inn at Wray, on the main road. A famous local event is a Maytime scarecrow festival.

Head into the village centre and turn left along the main street past the George & Dragon and the Holy Trinity church. *Dating from 1840, the Church House of 1694 stands alongside: just beyond is an ornate street lamp commemorating Queen Victoria's Golden Jubilee in 1887.* Just before the Post office/shop turn right up School Lane (signed Roeburndale West), and begin a steep climb of Dick Brow. *Take a well earned break to look back over the village:*

high beyond is Three Peaks Country. As the climb eases out look over to the right to see Hornby Castle rising out of the trees, with a massive Lakeland skyline beyond. A second steep pull precedes a junction with Moor Lane. _Over to the right is a major length of the Lune Valley._ Turn left, inevitably uphill, though the hard work is almost done. At a cattle-grid at Whit Moor Gate the moor is gained, and bracing strides reveal vast views over Roeburndale to the high moors. _Though this road start is not ideal it has few alternatives, but it's very peaceful and does at least get you off to a flier._

Striding out, several farms are passed. _These include Middle Wood, promoting environmentally aware building design and land use: it has a study centre and runs courses. Beyond the trench of Roeburndale, an array of 2000ft mountains ranging from Great Coum to Fountains Fell incorporate Yorkshire's Three Peaks. Passing Barkingate there are several novel features, including a stone circle formed from a collection of gateposts._ Only leave the road on reaching the first farm on the right. Turn up the drive to Thornbush, passing along the front of the house and then at the end, up to a gate. Entering a field a track heads away, though the way officially rises to

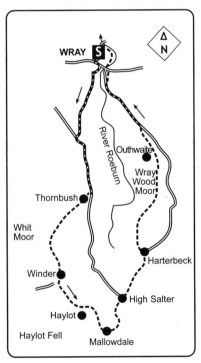

the top corner above a line of Scots Pine, where a gate puts you back on the track: it is easily overlooked in favour of remaining on the track to the foot of the trees before climbing alongside them.

Pass through the gate ahead, and with another just above, the track rises more gently left with a sunken way. When the track swings right to a gate, go straight on with the grassy groove to a wall ahead. Go left with it to locate a built-in stile, behind which cross the steep walls enclosing Warm Beck above its upper trees. Across, slant left up the rough pasture of Barkin to a gate in the far corner. At around 918ft/280m this section includes the walk's high point. A rough track heads away to the corner of a small plantation not shown on the map. Pass this to a minor brow and down to the enclosure of Hill Barn, just past which is Winder Farm. *This is an exposed old settlement - note the 1673 datestone above the door.* Its drive runs along to a road.

Turn left through a gate and down the road's accommodating verges, with Haylot Farm visible ahead. *Above it rises a moorland skyline featuring the cone of Mallowdale Pike.* Winding steeply down to cross Bladder Stone Beck, the road then re-ascends to the farm. Ignoring its continuation to the left, instead take a gate into the yard and almost at once another on the left into a field. Cross to a gate in the bottom right corner, and descend a small enclosure to a stile at the wall-foot. Below, a steep wooded bank falls to the winding Roeburn, while across to the right is Mallowdale Farm, with a deep valley intervening: the high moors draw close now.

Head along the bank high above the river, using a stile midway to step inside to enjoy a champagne moment. From here a super little path winds down the wooded slope, deep into the secretive confines to cross a footbridge on Mallow Gill. *Immediately upstream, a delectable watersmeet greets the eye. Forged beneath a green pyramid, this is a place to linger, and worth every step of that early road walking.* Penance is swift: from a stile beyond the bridge, a faint way zigzags up the steep bank to Mallowdale Farm. Keep left outside its confines, crossing to a stile to join its drive beyond the house. This winds down to Mallowdale Bridge amid newly planted trees, then doubles steeply back up the opposite slope to a barn. *Pause here to appraise Mallowdale's peerless setting under the edge of the moor.* Up to the right, meanwhile, is High Salter: advance as far as the cattle-grid ahead, but then take a stile on the right and ascend the field to the farming hamlet. Keep right of all buildings to a gate onto the Hornby Road or Salter's Way, here enjoying its final unsurfaced yards.

Turn down the road, but leave almost at once by a gate on the right. *Ahead, Ingleborough and friends reign supreme.* When the wall turns down go with it to a ladder-stile. Turn right to another then aim diagonally away for the far corner, but before reaching it bear left to a fence-stile. Resume to the wall and turn down it to a reedy corner where a stile gives access to a large, reedy pasture. With the buildings of Harterbeck ahead, bear right to a stile in a fence corner. Follow the fence along a minor bank to the top of High Buckbank Wood at a prominent knoll. This is another super moment: directly below is a substantial waterfall on Goodber Beck, deep in a rocky wooded ravine. Just upstream is a footbridge, and from the knoll you can also see the gentler upper falls. From the footbridge a green path slants left to a wall, which leads along to meet a track running to Harterbeck. It becomes enclosed at a slab footbridge/ford to emerge onto the roadhead at the farm entrance.

Turn right a few paces along the road to a cattle-grid on the left, where a track runs to another just ahead. Through this, leave the track and turn right along the fenceside. Through a gate at the end a track is joined: this runs down the fieldside to a barn. *More glorious views look, as ever, to majestic Ingleborough and also westwards over wooded Roeburndale.* From the ladder-stile here, continue to a stile in the wall ahead to enter a vast, moor-like pasture. Maintain this line on a fairly distinct way, through an old wall, past a lone tree and on to a wall-stile. Continue to a corner where a long, solid wall starts on the right. This remains for company, a long walk giving ample opportunity to enjoy wooded Roeburndale views. Over on the right terrain gives way to stony Wray Wood Moor, and at the far corner a gate leads you into a welcoming, slightly stony pasture.

The Wray cherub

To the right are open views across to Burn Moor beyond the intervening Hindburn Valley, while a reed-fringed pool makes up for the absence of reed-camouflaged Wray

Wood Moor Tarn over the wall. At the next corner a short-lived walled way is entered: at the end keep on to a drive serving the hamlet of Outhwaite to the left. Turn right over the cattle-grid but leave at once by a stile cleverly built into the wall corner. Head away, crossing a streamlet to accompany its deep-cut course down to a stile. Continue down to find a conspicuous stile in a tiny wall at the bottom, then bear right to a gate/stile onto a back road.

All that remains is to turn downhill, a good mile or so back into Wray. The way steepens and winds down through the wooded environs of Hunt's Gill Beck. Just beyond is a renovated former bobbin mill and a row of workers' cottages. *Past here Kitty Bridge offers a quick return to the village.* Remain on the road by the river to reach Wray Bridge, at the end of the wood noting a stile sending a short-cut field path to a stile at the end of a short terrace. *Built about 1780, Wray Bridge withstood the floods that wreaked havoc after a freak cloudburst on the moors in August 1967, causing the river to rise 20 feet in just 20 minutes. Its sturdiness only increased the damage as water banked up, and the little green caught the full fury of the devastation. A garden by surviving Bridge End is on the site of five houses that fell victim out of a row of six.* Across the bridge either return to the main street, noting on the right a plethora of old datestones, or turn down the green riverbank to see the Roeburn's confluence with the larger Hindburn. Continue downstream to return to the riverside area at the bridge, which replaced the humped Meal Bank Bridge swept away by the floods.

Upper Roeburndale from the farm track to Winder

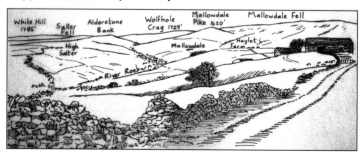

FOURSTONES

START Bentham   Grid ref. SD 667692

DISTANCE $5^3 4$ miles (9km)

ORDNANCE SURVEY MAPS
1:50,000
Landranger 98 - Wensleydale & Upper Wharfedale
1:25,000
Explorer OL41 - Forest of Bowland & Ribblesdale

ACCESS Start from the town centre. Car parks. Served by Leeds-Morecambe train, and Lancaster-Settle/Ingleton bus.

Gentle rambling around the ancient Forest of Mewith, with the walk's remarkable objective at its moorland summit

Bentham (properly High Bentham) is a bustling old market town on the northern limit of Bowland. Its true colours are shown by being part of Yorkshire, and its surroundings offer tantalizing panoramas of the mountains of Three Peaks Country, most notably mighty Ingleborough. This western outpost of England's premier county is situated just a dozen miles from Morecambe Bay. Shops and pubs abound, and a livestock market survives.

From the main street descend the road past the rail station to cross the bridge over the River Wenning. Turn sharp right on a driveway downstream. As it forks before the caravan park, bear left to the houses at Moulterbeck. Pass between the buildings and a gate, then turn left up the field to locate a stile into the wood. A lovely path climbs through narrow confines, passing a charming waterfall before emerging out of the trees at a stile. Continue up to a stile at a fence corner, going left on a broad track to the rear of the buildings at Brookhouse.

Through a gate at a ramshackle barn, take another in front and turn right up the field to a stile at the top. *Ingleborough makes a magnificent prospect behind, aided by less prominent Whernside and Penyghent.* Continue to a stile in a tiny section of wall, on to a gate at a fence corner, then on a fenceside to approach Bowker House. A muddy, enclosed way leads to the farm buildings, passing to their left and out on the drive. Cross straight over Mewith Lane to a gate just to the left, and climb two fields (intervening stile) to Flannagill on the skyline. From a stile onto its drive, turn along the house front and up to a stile in the garden wall - an alternative runs outside the garden. Entering the expansive grassy moorland of Bents, a gentle rise is made with the aid of sheeptrods. The Great Stone of Fourstones soon appears on the skyline ahead. This is your goal, and a couple of farm drives are crossed en route.

The Great Stone - locally known simply as the 'Big Stone' - is a quite remarkable feature, carried here by a glacier at the end of the Ice Age. Its name suggests there be three more about, but these are likely to have been much less grand. Fourteen hewn steps make an 'ascent' obligatory, its super panorama embracing a massive sweep of Three Peaks Country across the Wenning farmland. Nearer to hand, the Bowland moors cut off more distant prospects. At 787ft/240m this

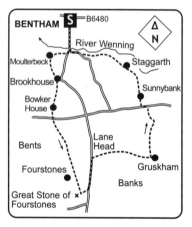

is, in every sense, the walk's high point. A path doubles back to the Slaidburn road, where panels entice motorists to take in the view.

The road is followed north towards Lane Head where it becomes enclosed at a cattle-grid, but before that turn right along a firm drive to the distinctive Fairfield House: indeed, you can cut across to it at any point. As the drive ends, cross the grassy ravine of Burbles Gill by a footbridge and head directly away on a path across the moorland of Banks. *This seems quite an expanse until you consider the vast sprawl of Burn Moor rising above, itself just one small corner of the great moorland massif of Bowland.*

Continuing east a hard track is met at a wall coming up from the left, and runs on to several houses. Pass one on your left to approach Gruskham, directly ahead. Here turn sharp left to a stile and descend the fieldside. Passing through a gate midway, at the bottom corner enter a short-lived, broad green way to emerge at an isolated house in a grand corner. Advance past a small orchard on the left to a massive barn, and follow the drive out as it drops pleasantly down to meet Mewith Lane. Go briefly left and turn down Sunnybank Farm drive on the right. Pass behind the farmhouse into the yard, then take a gate on the left from where a track slants diagonally down the field to a gate. Through this, turn down the hedgeside to a wall-stile at the bottom. Drop towards the wooded bank below, and bear left along its top to a stone bench and information panel. These overlook a gorgeous wooded bank falling steeply to the River Wenning, a super spot for a final break.

Resume slanting down to a gate, then curve over the tapering field on a thin path to the farm at Staggarths. A novel stile enters the yard. At the end, don't follow the drive out past the house, but go right through a gate then sharp left across the field to a kissing-gate close by the river. Advance on the riverside, around a sharp bend to a gate in a wall. While an unofficial path remains with the river, the right of way goes left along the wall to a stile at the end, then across a large field to rejoin the river at the end. Through a wall-stile, cross to a gateway at a wall-cum-hedge corner, and then follow the latter away to a stile onto a back road. Turn right on this to quickly return to the bridge on the edge of town, to finish the walk as you began.

The Great Stone of Fourstones

HINDBURN COUNTRY

START Lowgill   Grid ref. SD 653647

DISTANCE 6$\frac{1}{2}$ miles (10$\frac{1}{2}$km)

ORDNANCE SURVEY MAPS
1:50,000
Landranger 97 - Kendal to Morecambe
Landranger 98 - Wensleydale & Upper Wharfedale
1:25,000
Explorer OL41 - Forest of Bowland & Ribblesdale

ACCESS Start from the centre of the hamlet. Limited parking on the wider sections of road above the houses; or alternatively there is a lay-by opposite the church (at the end of the walk, GR 653653). Further parking just downstream from Mill Bridge.

> An off the beaten track excursion entirely within the upper valley of the unsung River Hindburn, with much of interest in and around its only hamlet of Lowgill

Lowgill is a small community whose Rose & Crown inn survived into the 1970s. A Methodist church of 1866 sits on a lawn that enjoys a brief spell as a sea of snowdrops, while Lowgill House sports an 18th century datestone. Head up the main street past a tiny green bearing a seat, war memorial and phone box, and up the narrowing up-dale road. *With much holly in evidence in the hedge-rows, already you enjoy fine views over the wooded Hindburn Valley, with high moors enclosing the dale.* Crossing Bull Gill, keep straight on at a junction at the hamlet of Ivah. Through a couple of kinks the road emerges to run on to a sharp bend. *The sections immediately before and just along from here are on the line of the Roman road from Ribchester to Over Burrow in the Lune Valley.*

As the road turns downhill, advance straight on a drive to Swans. Take the gate to the barn left of the house, then straight on through another and up the tiny bank to a gate behind. Beyond it a faint green track runs above a gnarled hedge, with grand views as you drop to a grassy bridge and bridle-gate at the end. Advance on through an old wall and along to a brow. *Below is a prospect of the confluence of Middle Gill and Whitray Beck in lovely wooded surrounds.* Whitray Farm forms a distinct objective directly ahead. Continuing, descend left to a bridle-gate by a boulder at the base of a section of wall, then drop sharp right from it to a footbridge on Whitray Beck. Tackling the steep bank behind, bear slightly left as a faint, hollowed way leads on to a wall corner, and a track soon forms to lead directly up two fieldsides to Whitray Farm.

Continue through the yard and out on the drive, turning right along this moorfoot road. *This is the high point of the walk at just 785ft/239m: on the left the slopes of Whitray Fell front many untracked Bowland miles, while ahead is a glimpse of Mallowdale Pike overtopping a moor-*

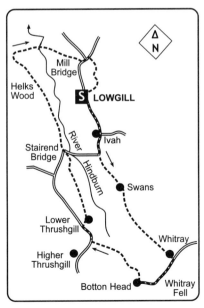

land ridge. After crossing the burbling moorland stream of Middle Gill the road ends at Botton Head Farm. Enter the yard and go immediately right to a gate. A track aims directly away down a field centre, on a tongue dividing the two upper arms of Hindburndale. Through a gate at the bottom it traces the fieldside to a gate in the bottom corner. Going left through the gate, your green road can be seen zigzagging up the opposite slope. A steeper descent finds Botton Bridge hidden in lovely surrounds.

Up the other side the track enjoys a delectable grassy zigzag, with a more solid older surface evident. From a gate at the top look back over dalehead country to Whitray and Botton Head, then advance to join a road through the fields. Up to the left is Higher Thrushgill beneath a sizeable plantation. Two minutes along to the right, and becoming enclosed at a gate, turn down a drive to Lower Thrushgill. Go left through a gate to pass left of the original house (1798 datestone at the back), along its lawn-side and a short-lived green way to a stile into a field. Head directly away along a minor tongue, on a straight line through several stiles in reedy pastures.

The day's first wall-stile leads to a vast, reedy pasture. Continue down, keeping a wooded bank on the right until it subsides. As the trees end turn down to the right to approach a sharp crook of the river, with a gate onto a road just to the left. Note, just before it, a disturbing example of the erosive powers of a normally modest stream. On the right the Hindburn flows under Stairend Bridge, while you go left to accompany it down to a sharp bend after crossing Mill Beck. By this confluence pass through a gate on the right.

Entering a reedy riverside pasture, a track runs on to cross a stream at the far end beneath an attractive wooded bank. Keep on through a longer pasture to a gate at the end. Here leave the river by bearing left to another gate where a grassy track climbs through a long-collapsed wall. It now rises faintly through colourful country to a ruinous barn. *Note the prospect of Lowgill directly across the main valley.* Up to the left is the great bowl of Helks Wood. From a gate beyond the barn, traces of a wall lead across to a notch in the bracken slope, reached via a gate accessing new tree planting. A further gate in a line of trees behind sees you up the small bank behind. Advance to cross a deep wooded beck before slanting steeply left to a gate before a crumbling barn. Pass along the front to a gate at the end, then on to a gate just above a restored barn.

Cross again to the edge of a deeper wooded stream, then turn down its near side. At the bottom corner a wall-stile admits to Over Houses Great Wood, and a grand little path winds down a dense bluebell bank to approach the river. Through a hurdle-stile at the bottom turn downstream a short way to a footbridge across it. *This is a gorgeous little spot to break, with the end now fairly close. Like its neighbour the Roeburn, the Hindburn takes its name from the deer that commonly frequented these parts.*

Turn downstream to a kissing-gate, and a flight of steps up a wooded bank to a stile. In the field above, a faint grassy track rises to a gate by a barn, rising again through a higher field. Instead of going through the gate at the top, opt for a gateway in the hedge to its left, and head along the top of the initially wooded bank to a gate at the far side. *The Roman road is crossed yet again here.* The gate admits to Lowgill Lane: turn right for a direct return to the hamlet, otherwise go left down to Mill Bridge, a lovely spot. Just across it turn up a narrow lane between buildings, and just above a cobbled hairpin is the drive to Lowgill church.

The church of the Good Shepherd is a stout edifice, its great tower appearing to rest on groaning walls. The present building dates only from 1888: its stained glass reflects its location and name, eminently suitable for this isolated farming country. A stile enters the field parallel to the church drive, continuing through a gate at the end to a small enclosure adjacent to the churchyard. If visiting the church, a gate out of the yard corner leads to this enclosure. This leads to the churchgoers' path from the village. *Just behind the church is the former school: not merely closed like so many rural schools, but only replaced, as you shall soon see.*

Drawing level with the old school, don't go to the stile at the end, but turn down the steep bank on a partly stepped path to a footbridge in a wooded dell of the Hindburn. Up the other side stay with the right-hand fence, a wall taking over at the top to run to a corner. As a fence takes over turn through the gate and along a part enclosed way to approach the hamlet: the modern school is just down to the right. At a small housing development, advance to a bridle-gate to the edge of a farmyard then turn right onto the road.

***The Good Shepherd,
Lowgill***

WHELP STONE CRAG

START *Giggleswick* **Grid ref.** *SD 803628*

DISTANCE *9 miles (14¹2km)*

ORDNANCE SURVEY MAPS
1:50,000
Landranger 98 - Wensleydale & Upper Wharfedale
Landranger 103 - Blackburn & Burnley
1:25,000
Explorer OL41 - Forest of Bowland & Ribblesdale

ACCESS *Start from Giggleswick station on the Leeds-Morecambe line. There is a car park here, and a lay-by just back along the road. The village centre and Settle are a good mile up the road past the Old Station pub. Both villages are also served by bus from Skipton and Ingleton/Lancaster.*

A richly varied excursion from the edge of the Dales into some fascinating countryside, with a fine landmark as the objective

Any walk starting from the Settle area normally makes for its more obvious Dales attractions, yet Bowland's boundaries also reach this way, and this fine walk takes in a familiar landmark - though few will know it by name. Whelp Stone Crag is a prominent feature from the busy A65: heading north from Long Preston, its flat-topped outline sits distinctly on the skyline across the Ribble.

From the station use the steps down to the by-pass, and take the side road under the railway line. Passing Swaw Beck Farm it rises to a junction. Take the narrower branch left, and in 100 yards keep left up a rough, walled lane. *Look back to enjoy the start of near permanent views over the Ribble to Settle's limestone hills, backed by Rye Loaf Hill and Fountains Fell.* The lane runs into a field. *From the gate look back to find Penyghent entering the scene above Giggleswick Quarry, while further left Ingleborough's classic outline appears in splendid isolation. Also prominent is the copper dome of Giggleswick School chapel.* Cross to the far corner where a stile leads to a gate onto the old green way of Cocket Lane. Turn up its partly restored course, still encountering damp moments as it accommodates a small stream. A good prospect of Rome Crag is seen across to the right. Emerging into a broadening, rough pasture at the end, rise by the left-hand wall to a brow. *With stony ground extending west from the Rome Crag group, here is a first forward prospect, colourful open country promising much.*

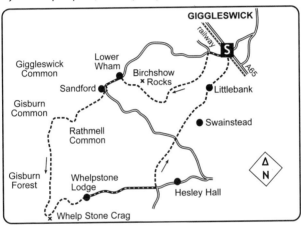

As the wall turns away, Cocket Moss appears below. Bear left above the moss - fenced to deter kamikaze sheep - and drop to a gate in the bottom corner beneath the scattered boulders of Moor Close Crag. Here a mercifully solid embanked track bridges the mire to a bouldery brow behind. Continue away to a minor brow just short of a wall. Here turn right on excellent turf to a gate at the end with distinctive Birchshow Rocks ahead - a splendid array of cragginess. Head away with the wall, as it ends keep on beneath the rocks to a gate at the far end. Advance past the last straggling rocks to an old wall, then bear left past a wall corner to a gate in the far corner. Cross a small enclosure to a gate onto a back road.

Turn left past Lower Wham, emerging onto open common to approach Sandford Farm. A corner of this pocket moor can be cut to drop onto the road going left past the farm, quickly reaching a gate where it emerges onto a greater swathe where Giggleswick and Rathmell Commons meet. Turn right up the wallside, with faint sheeptrods through largely dry, reedy terrain. At a small kink in the wall a reedier, moist patch is encountered. Bear gently away from the wall, locating a thin way rising steadily to run a distinct course beneath a bracken bank. Ahead now is the forest edge, and the crest of Whelp Stone Crag appears. Striding happily along, take a clearer right branch slanting up through bracken to the prominent ruin of a shooting lodge. *Alongside is a lichen-encrusted stone trough, with a cool, gurgling spring behind the far corner wall. With a few rocks scattered about, this is a grand spot for a break.*

Though the path ends, a thin trod takes up the reins, on beneath scattered rocks to reveal the knoll of Foxholes Crag just ahead. Cross to it to find an array of boulders offering playful scrambling and some shelter. On the adjacent knoll is the ruin of a stone hut. *Vast rolling moors lead the eye north to Ingleborough.* Revealed just below you is a narrow neck where a marshy stream escapes from Deep Moss, the perfect place to cross to the small outcrop behind. Then simply ascend the slope above and bear left just before the brow to set a bee-line for Whelp Stone Crag.

Winter on Whelp Stone Crag, looking to Ingleborough

Through scattered smaller rocks, remain on this domed, largely dry ground as you cross Gisburn Common towards the near forest corner. A faint green track forms to run towards it, becoming a well made way rising to the wood edge. *Turn to savour this location, ensconced in upland colour.* Through the gateway, step over the fence on the left and head up the forest edge. Before long you'll find better progress outside the old wall. While the crag increases in dominance, the Bowland fells are revealed over to the right. Underneath the nearest craggy bluff the way rises slightly and swings right towards the forest, briefly entering it at a corner-stile at a wall-end. At a collapsed wall junction at the end turn left, still within these upper plantings to the western rim of the Crag.

Though Whelp Stone Crag's crest is just above, first consider dropping right through the wall-gap to find yourself beneath a stern craggy brow bristling with scrambling potential, at the base of which reposes a discarded millstone. To gain the top, remain on the clearer path slanting up to a gate where wall and fence meet. Through it, simply ascend left onto the crest. At 1217ft/371m the summit is an extensive viewpoint. Its OS column surmounts a small outcrop, though one is naturally drawn to the craggy northern rim. *The panorama includes Bowland's steep slopes and rounded tops beyond Stocks Reservoir, Pendle Hill with the South Pennine heights beyond, and an array of Dales mountains nearer to hand.*

A thin path runs east along this well-defined edge, and a wall comes up to usher you to a gateway in a wall ahead. Either slant right down to the wall below, and on a track to a gate by a stone sheepfold, or opt to maintain higher ground as long as possible, over one bouldery knoll and on to the spiky end. *This is a smashing viewpoint for Dales limestone country, featuring Ingleborough, Norber, Moughton, Giggleswick Scar, Penyghent, Fountains Fell, Settle and its distinctive hills such as Warrendale Knotts.* From here double back right, contouring around the edge past a sizeable quarried crag and down a slanting rake to drop precisely to the gate by the sheep-pen. From it cross to a gateway opposite, though don't pass through but bear left with the wall. From its corner advance down the pasture to a gate in a similar corner.

Through the gate a grassy track descends to Whelpstone Lodge. Head out along the access track, soon becoming surfaced. Known as Old Oliver Lane, the road is followed for a further mile, traffic-free, downhill and with grand views. Passing through a small wooded clough, a junction is reached. Go briefly left, bound for Rathmell. *Opposite the drive just ahead, a milestone at the base of the wall bears a weathered inscription, referring to the three miles to Tosside Chapel, as Tosside was once better known.*

Here turn left up the drive to Hesley Cottage, passing to the right and up to a gate in a fence. Rise to a wall corner above and take a stile in the continuing fence, then bear gently right up onto the brow. Pass through a wall-stile in front and advance to the next one ahead, then on again to a stile onto a surfaced access road. From a stile opposite, slant left to locate a squeezer-stile in the descending wall. Slant down the bouldery pasture to the rear of a barn, and take the left-hand gate to descend a large pasture to the foot of the wall on the left. Here a little footbridge crosses Rathmell Beck in a pleasant setting. Rise directly up the bank to another stile at the far corner. On through an oval enclosure, bear right and up by wall and fenceside to a gate onto a back road.

Go briefly left then turn right along a superb green way between walls, Swainstead Raike. *On the brow Settle returns to the scene beneath its hills.* At the end the track emerges into a no-man's-land, meeting a track just ahead. Bear briefly right on it, but then cut back left to a gate just above the highest trees lining the tiny stream. A green rake bears right above the beck, then a path-less way runs atop the wooded bank. This big stony pasture is Coney Garth, a rabbit warren. Towards the bottom bear a little left to a wall-stile into a pocket oakwood. Bear left out of it to contour on to a fence-stile, then keep straight on across the large, sloping field to approach the impressive house of Littlebank.

Littlebank's drive is joined but not followed, as a stile admits to the wooded outer garden. Descend the overgrown garden foot to a kissing-gate in the far corner. Drop left down the field to a stile where wall and fence meet.Cross to a wall-stile in front of the farm at Littlebank Barn ahead, and across a small enclosure between the barns and house, head directly away with a wall on your left. Through a gate at the end bear slightly left to a wall-stile, then advance over a low brow with the wall, taking a stile near the end to cross a field corner to the next. Cross to another into the last field, with the station just ahead. A stile at the far corner leads to the road under the railway bridge to return to the station.

BOWLAND KNOTTS

START *Cross of Greet Bridge*   *Grid ref. SD 702590*

DISTANCE *6 miles (9¹2km)*

ORDNANCE SURVEY MAPS
1:50,000
Landranger 98 - Wensleydale & Upper Wharfedale
Landranger 103 - Blackburn & Burnley
1:25,000
Explorer OL41 - Forest of Bowland & Ribblesdale

ACCESS *Start from the car park by the bridge, 4¹2 miles north of Slaidburn on the Bentham road.* • *OPEN ACCESS - see page 9.*

> *A relatively easy circuit of relatively wild country*

   Cross of Greet Bridge straddles the youthful River Hodder as it tumbles down the fells of its birth. From here you can already survey much of the route, including Catlow Fell and Bowland Knotts. Start by crossing the bridge to a kissing-gate onto the open fell, on which you will remain for almost the entire walk. Cross the sidestream of Near Costy Clough and a thin trod winds up the bracken bank to very quickly meet a grassy shooters' track. Turn right on this as it starts to slant up the fellside. You now have a choice of ways for the next long half-mile.
   Driest option remains on this track rising to a pair of cabins, then slant more steeply down the colourful fellside to reach Far Costy Clough in front of the former Jumbles Quarry. Alternatively, within a minute of joining the track, bear off right on an initially faint way which can be identified as the bed of a former narrow gauge steam railway. *This was constructed in 1924 (extended from an earlier line) to transport quarried stone for the building of the*

Stocks dam - there is further evidence in the form of decaying wooden sleepers. The old way runs a direct course at the slightest of gradients well above the beck. It falters in marshy terrain just short of Far Costy Clough in front of the old quarry. *Immediately above the quarry, Far Costy Clough is a hugely colourful little side valley.*

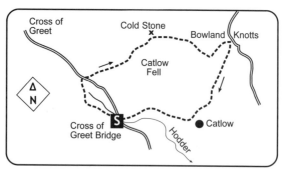

Cross the stream and a thin trod ascends the heathery bank to look down on the old site. *A forlorn steam crane, used to load stone onto the railway waggons, survives alongside bouldery spoil heaps. Note the diverted course of the stream into a pool within the site, also surviving rails in the bed of the stream.* On leaving slant down to the Hodder, and a little further upstream cross it: with the wall to your right rise onto the Cross of Greet road. Turn right over the cattle-grid and recommence climbing, now among scattered rocks on inviting, steep grassy slopes. *The view south opens out to reveal Stocks Reservoir and Pendle Hill, while the moorland road climbs through colourful country to Cross of Greet.* A massive boulder across the wall marks the top, from where turn right along the moor edge, traversing above the modest scattering of boulders. *The old tramway is clearly highlighted below.* The rocks fade as the edge swings left, revealing distinctive Penyghent and Fountains Fell peering through the watershed gap you will shortly be passing through, with Bowland Knotts up to its right.

For now, simply contour around the moorland slope, before long seeing a wall ahead. Join this watershed wall and drop the short distance to the Cold Stone beside it. *Before this you will have found Ingleborough and then Whernside adding to the panorama of Dales peaks. The Cold Stone is a massive piece of rock preceded by a row of lesser ones. It offers ample scope for bouldering routes, as well as some shelter beneath the overhang. The trig point on Bowland Knotts can be seen across the depression ahead, fronting the jagged skyline of the Knotts.* Resume with the wall as it runs down to the dip at Copy Nook, passing through an intervening wall and ascending the other side, soon reaching better terrain at the onset of Bowland Knotts. Towards the top bear right to reach the Ordnance Survey column, at 1411ft/430m the summit of the walk. *Bowland Knotts is a delight, as ahead a range of craggy knolls extends well beyond the unseen Clapham-Slaidburn road. Immediately below your edge is an extensive marsh, a little beyond which is similarly extensive Gisburn Forest. Certainly it is the Dales skyline to the north that holds all the aces. A prostrate boundary stone inscribed 'C' is found at the nearby wall corner.*

Advance through an old wall and over various knolls to reach a wall ahead, where drop right to a gate. You can opt to pass through to the road to explore the continuing Knotts, but the actual route instead follows the broad track back to the right. Almost dead straight and well made, this crosses the moss edge to a gateway in a wall corner at the end. Pass through to be greeted by a glorious prospect of Stocks Reservoir and Upper Hodder country. Instead of following the grassy track down the rough pasture, slant right, soon finding a reedy, sunken way with an adjacent grassy trod dropping to a prominent barn. Here a crumbling wall leads down to the intake wall below. Pass through the gate in it, just above Catlow Farm, and slant down to the opposite corner where a gate takes you from the walk's only grassy pasture back into reedy terrain.

A good track slants down from here to join the Hodder, at the confluence with Keasden Holes amid a barrage of unsightly fencing. Just upstream, the track fords this tiny inflowing stream. From the gate beyond, don't follow the rising track but maintain a level course beneath the bank. A generally clear grassy way runs through reeds to rejoin the Hodder, and a thin path follows this upstream to a gateway alongside sheepfolds. Reed-filled and unused, this elaborate arrangement is in excellent condition. Resume along the bank, noting a similar sheepfold on the other bank before running along to reach the finish via a moist area.

WALK LOG

WALK	DATE	NOTES
1		
2		
3		
4		
5		
6		
7		
8		
9		
10		
11		
12		
13		
14		
15		
16		
17		
18		
19		
20		
21		
22		

USEFUL ADDRESSES

The Ramblers
2nd Floor, Camelford House, 87-89 Albert Embankment, London SE1 7BR
• 020-7339 8500

Lancashire Countryside Service (Forest of Bowland AONB)
Guild House, Cross Street, Preston PR1 8RD
• 01772-531473

Bowland Visitor Centre
Beacon Fell, near Goosnargh PR3 2NL
• 01995-640557

Tourist Information Centres
Council Offices, Church Walk **Clitheroe** BB7 2RA • 01200-425566

Discovery Centre, High Street **Garstang** PR3 1FU • 01995-602125

The Guildhall, Lancaster Road **Preston** PR1 1HT • 01772-253731

Town Hall, Cheapside **Settle** BD24 9EJ • 01729-825192

29 Castle Hill **Lancaster** LA1 1YN • 01524-32878

Station Road **Bentham** LA2 7LF • 015242-62549

Lancashire and Blackpool Tourist Board
St George's House, St George's Street, Chorley PR7 2AA
• 01257-226600

Open Access
Open Access Contact Centre, PO Box 725, Belfast BT1 3YL
Helpline • 0845-100 3298, *or* www.countrysideaccess.gov.uk

Public Transport Information
Traveline • 0870 608 2608
National Rail Enquiries • 08457-484950

INDEX
walk number refers